HOW TO FACE INTERVIEW KNOW SKILL TO SELECT IN INTERVIEW

SATISH KUMAR

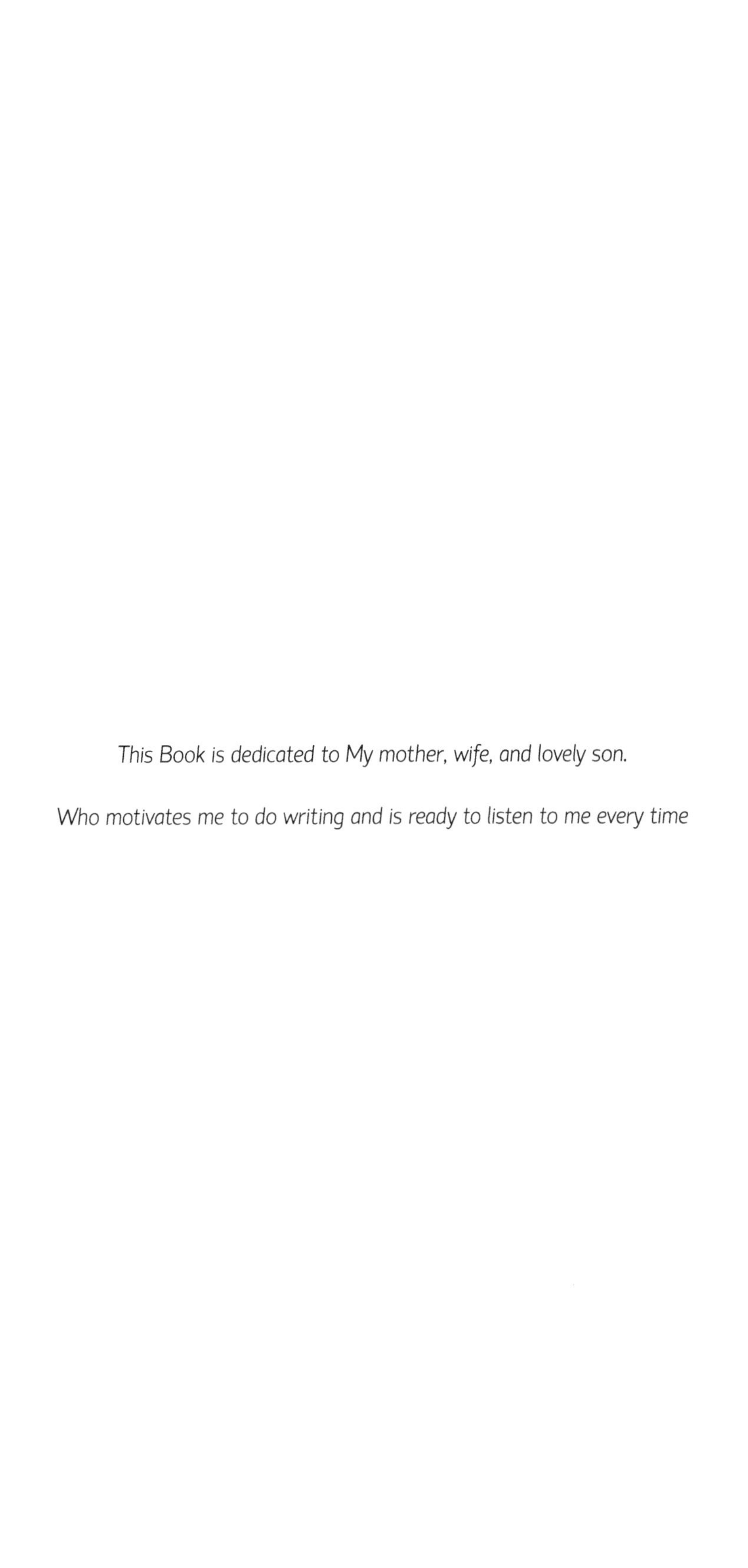

This Book is dedicated to My mother, wife, and lovely son.

Who motivates me to do writing and is ready to listen to me every time

Contents

CHAPTER ONE

Introduction

I am writing this book for those who are looking for job, who are already in job and want to change job role for career growth.

If you are looking for a job or want to change job then you have a good book which will help you to clear your interview.

As we know without cracking the interview, we cannot get a good job. We have some common qualities and skills for selection in the interview on the basis of which we can select.

This book will give you the knowledge of how to prepare for the interview and what qualities to look for in the interview to get the job. This book contains the knowledge that will help you to improve yourself.

In organizations or companies, interviews are generally conducted to test the interviewee, check their domain knowledge, check their skills, check their behaviour and attitude, and many other aspects that affect the organizational performance. are necessary to meet the requirements.

Only after proper assessment the interviewee is selected for the job role. Failing in job interview does not mean that you are incapable of doing the work, you do not need to worry about it, still you have to work on your flaws, try to polish your skill-set, understand that you Where do you fall short, how can you fill the gap, what are the measures you need to take, and finally, the things you need to succeed in the interview. Self-assessment plays a major role here.

To evaluate an interviewer, only one type of interview is not followed by the interviewer rather they evaluate the interviewer by testing them with different types of interviews. Because it becomes important to prepare yourself for different types of interviews. But before that, you should know what are the types of interviews and how they are conducted.

CHAPTER TWO

What is Interview

Firstly, we will discuss what is interview.

The interview is a formal meeting between two people (Interviewer and interviewee). The interview is conducted to ask questions and obtain information from the interviewee. An Interviewer is the one who asks questions and an interviewee is who answers the questions.

An interview is a structured conversation where one participant asks questions, and the other provides answers. In common parlance, the word "interview" refers to a one-on-one conversation between an interviewer and an interviewee. The interviewer asks questions to which the interviewee responds, usually providing information. That information may be used or provided to other audiences immediately or later. This feature is common to many types of interviews – a job interview or interview with a witness to an event may have no other audience present at the time, but the answers will be later provided to others in the employment or investigative process. An interview may also transfer information in both directions.

Interviews usually take place face-to-face and in person but the parties may instead be separated geographically, as in videoconferencing or telephone interviews. Interviews almost always involve spoken conversation between two or more parties. In some instances, a "conversation" can happen between two persons who type their questions and answers.

Interviews can be unstructured, free-wheeling and open-ended conversations without predetermined plan or prearranged questions. One form of unstructured interview is a focused interview in which the interviewer consciously and consistently guides the conversation so that the interviewee's responses do not stray from the main research topic or idea. Interviews can also be highly structured conversations in which specific questions occur in a specified order. They can follow diverse formats; for example, in a ladder interview, a respondent's answers typically guide subsequent interviews, with the object being to explore a respondent's subconscious motives. Typically, the interviewer has some way of recording the information that is gleaned from the interviewee, often by keeping notes with a pencil and paper, or with a video or audio recorder. Interviews usually have a limited duration, with a beginning and an ending.

The traditionally two-person interview format, sometimes called a one-on-one interview, permits direct questions and follow-ups, which enables an interviewer to better gauge the accuracy and relevance of responses. It is a flexible arrangement in the sense that subsequent questions can be tailored to clarify earlier answers. Further, it eliminates possible distortion due to other parties being present.

Face to face interviewing helps both parties to interact and form a connection, and understand the other. Further, face to face interview sessions can be more enjoyable

CHAPTER THREE

Why Interviews Are an Important Part of The Recruitment Process

Interviews are an important part of the recruitment process because they can help HR professionals meet a variety of candidates and determine which one is right for their company's needs. Additionally, interviews can help you identify prospective employees who align with your company's goals and culture. You can also use an interview to:

Evaluate a candidate's work experience

In an interview, you can evaluate a candidate's qualifications, work experience and industry knowledge by asking targeted questions. The candidates' responses can help you identify who has a background that best aligns with your company's goals. Learning what skills and experience a candidate has can also help you determine if you may need to provide additional training to a candidate after hiring them.

Introduce a candidate to the company

During an interview, consider introducing candidates to the leaders of your organization. This can help you determine how they may form relationships in your company. It can also help you see how well they might fit into your company's culture.

Assess a candidate's hard and soft skills

Interviewing a candidate can help you determine their proficiency in various hard and soft skills. To evaluate their soft skills, you could ask questions about communication, problem-solving and teamwork. For positions that require technical skills, you might incorporate a hard skills test to determine a candidate's ability to perform a specific task, such as using Microsoft Excel.

Discover the most qualified candidates

Since interviews provide you with an opportunity to analyze a potential employee's experience, skills and professional background, they can help you discover the candidates who are best qualified for the position. This may assist you in choosing the right candidates to advance to the next stage of the hiring process. Additionally, it can expedite the recruitment process and help fill essential positions at your company quickly.

Social behaviour is analysed:

Another advantage of taking interviews is that the social behaviour of the individual is analysed. When a person speaks, his body language, the words he or she use are assessed and the basic etiquette are counted.

So, among many others, this is also one of the important reasons.

To get the best output for the company:

The company will be able to get the best output only when the employees are capable of achieving the targets.

So, if the employees themselves are not capable of doing the work the company demands, then how come the company will survive in such a tough competition in the market.

Now, to make the company efficient enough to fight and stay in the competition, it ought to choose the applicants who are capable and able to work hard.

Selecting a suitable person:

The company runs well when the candidates who are working in there are suitable for the company.

If not, then the company throws them out of the company. So, before reaching to such a rude level, the companies prefer not to reach to such level and prevent this situation as it is both embarrassing for the company and for the employee.

So, to prevent all this, interview plays an important role in the selection process.

Things an Interviewer Looks for During a Job Interview

Are you wondering what an interviewer looks for during an interview, or what you should do to get him to like you? Is there some secret to figuring out if the interview is going well or something else you can do to ensure that it does?

While you're in the interview hot seat watching for clues from your interviewer, he or she is busy watching you – looking for their own clues. Interviewers look for things they want to hear in your answers, or ways you handle yourself during the interview, or simply some sign that shows them what you might be like if you worked for them.

So I thought it might help you to know what kinds of things I specifically look for, and what I want to hear when I interview job candidates:

1. Do you actually answer the questions I ask?

Preparing for an interview ahead of time is really important. By all means, spend time looking at what kinds of questions might be asked and how to handle them. And practice, practice, practice.

But when it comes to the interview itself, listen carefully in the moment and answer the actual questions asked. I've had people come to interviews so overly prepared with canned answers that they try to use their memorized answers even if it's not exactly what was asked.

So listen to the whole question and respond naturally. If you jump ahead to practice your answer in your head while the interviewer is still talking, that's a big turnoff. Trust yourself and find your own words. Be conversational. It will help you connect with the interviewer, which is what you want to do.

2. What's your body language telling me?

Are you slouching? Relaxed is good, slouching is bad. Sit up straight, looking professional and yet as natural as possible. Also, be aware of any fidgets or extraneous body movements (tapping your finger or foot, clicking a pen) that can distract the interviewer from your words.

And don't forget to add a warm smile as you speak, again in a natural way. Grinning wildly throughout is only good if you're applying for a job as a smiley face. ?

By the way ... if you're nervous, don't assume that's a negative. We expect job candidates to be nervous. Just practice a lot beforehand, be yourself during the interview, and remember to meet the interviewer's eyes with that warm smile. Most likely you'll begin to relax – at least enough to do your best, which is all we ask.

3. What kind of eye contact are you making with me?

This is so important, yet for many job candidates difficult. Look me in the eyes when you speak – also when I ask you a question. If your eyes are darting around the room, you may look bored or uneasy in your own answers.

Again, as with the smile, you don't want to overdo it and create a staring contest. But easy eye contact during the conversational exchanges can help create that connection.

4. Are you showing me your real self?

Whether you're using canned answers or spontaneous answers, are you telling me what you think I want you to say or the real story based on who you are and the experiences you've had so far? You want to come to the interview 100% familiar with how you match the job.

Use your answers – answers based in truth – to paint the picture of a great match as best as possible. You do this using your career story – the unifying story you hopefully created to write your resume and cover letter.

I've had job candidates giving me only the part they think I want to see, and they come off phony or one-dimensional. And they just don't connect well with me or the other interviewers. If I think there's enough there, I try other ways to get them to open up to us, but many interviewers won't go that far.

5. Do you understand the job you're interviewing for?

This may seem so obvious, but I've interviewed people who didn't seem to know what the job entailed, even though they applied for it. Of course, you can't know everything about it.

Asking what the job is like on a daily basis is a valid question for you to ask at the end of the interview. But at the very least review the job description and look up anything you aren't completely familiar with.

6. Did you take time to learn about us?

In addition to researching the job, you need to research the company. What is the business all about? What are the specialties of the division / department you're interviewing with?

Use the internet to find out all you can – even possibly the names of people who work there. Then put together a picture of who they are, as best you can, again looking for ways that you and the company match.

One question interviewer like to ask is "What do you know about us?" Your research will help you prepare for that, too, helping you shape your answers and even how you dress for the interview.

7. Do you have the skills to do the job?

Hopefully, you checked out the job description ahead of time and can show evidence during the interview that you really have the skills. Some companies have special interviews and/ or tests to make sure, so be prepared.

And if there's anything they're looking for that you haven't used in a while or only know a little, by all means brush up on them before the interview!

8. Do you have the personality to do the job?

This is an important part of an interviewer's job. If the job calls for lots of people contact and public interactions, we don't want someone who seems especially shy.

But conversely, if the job takes place in a cubicle with almost no outside interaction, an extrovert might be bored.

9. Do you have reasonable expectations?

Employers not only want to know if you're a good fit for the job, but they're looking to make sure the job will be a good fit for you. An unhappy employee isn't good for anyone. And no employer wants to go through the hiring process again too soon.

While most employers want you to look to grow both horizontally and vertically within their company, it's also important that we get a sense you understand what the position is and isn't ... and how quickly any kind of advancement can be reasonably expected. Something you might want to ask about if this is your concern.

10. Would you fit in with our company and culture?

There isn't too much you can do about this. It's just something interviewers look for and think about during an interview. Even if you give the best interview ever, they may know something about the job or company that you don't – and they may be saving you both a bad experience. Again, just be yourself. It pays off in the long run.

A side note: While you might be at the interview prep stage for a particular job, it's best to continue to apply for other jobs (in case the one you are going to interview for does not work out). You can write a new resume for another job application (or tailor an existing resume) using our professional Resume Builder, which helps you get the work done in no time at all.

11. Are you adaptable / flexible?

Employers often use behavioural questions, where interviewers ask you how you handled things in the past, to assess your ability to respond to new situations with ease and success.

If you prepare your jobs experience stories well – things you've managed to improve or solve or help get done – you'll present a picture of someone who does rise to the occasion without bringing their own rigidity into the picture.

12. Are you resourceful?

Once again, your job experience stories (sometimes even life experience stories where appropriate) will help them see that you can manage to get things done without everything being handed to you on a silver platter.

13. Are you high maintenance?

Some job candidates come in with complaints on their faces about having to wait too long or not being able to bring their parents (yes really). Or they've called / emailed with lots of questions ahead of time. Not good.

And during the interview, the way you tell a story can show if you expect way too much from others (without pitching in yourself) and see things mostly from your own point of view. High maintenance is a big red flag.

14. Are you a problem solver?

We love these. Of course, you want to wait until you've gathered all the facts and are really sure there is a problem to solve. I've seen people come into interviews ready to fix the company – sure that their ideas would win them the job.

Stories about how you solved problems in the workplace are very good. But trying to improve the company while you're still in the interview process – not good.

[NOTE: If by slim chance they do ask you how you'd improve the company, base your answer on facts you've gathered during your research and not conclusions you've jumped to. Focus on steps you'd take to gather what you need to know. And show respect for current management / staff and what you can't possibly know.

15. Are you someone who respects management?

As mentioned above, a company wants to know that you're someone who will work well with managers and respect the company's mission and culture. If your answers include stories about how you were smarter than management and saved the day, this won't come across well.

Even if management was terrible, always tell your stories in a way that makes you look resourceful and capable, while not putting others down. Also ... do your research ahead of time to make sure you really are in synch with this company. No sense getting an unwelcome surprise after you start.

16. Are you a self-starter?

While companies want you to work well with management, they also want to know you won't just twiddle your thumbs and wait to be told everything.

I always look for clues that the person can operate independently, while still respecting the management structure and co-workers. Not that you can always figure this out in an interview.

17. Do you initiate useful change?

As mentioned before, most companies' welcome employees who are looking for ways to improve things – better quality products, more efficient processes, saving them money. But they aren't looking for someone just spinning out lots of ideas without focusing on what they were hired to do.

So, when you talk about the improvements you've made, look for work-based examples that, if possible, relate to the job you want now.

18. Do you know who you are and what you really want?

Sounds so simple. But if your answers and stories seem to touch on too many disconnected things, you may be presenting a picture that is too disjointed to leave an impression the employer feels solid about. We are too complex to fully present ourselves in a single job interview. Don't even try.

Be real and be natural, of course. But give them the pieces that help create that unified story we talked about earlier – one that matches the job you're applying for.

This means taking the time beforehand to really think about yourself and the job – and how the two come together as a result of your past experiences, skills, abilities and personality. If you know this well, then your answers will flow more naturally.

19. Do you know your own resume?

Again, so obvious. Yet folks come into an interview not having looked at their resume in a while. And I've had people have to think a bit when I ask them about something right there on the resume, they sent me.

Please give yourself some time to look at it before you arrive at the interview. You should also review it carefully when preparing stories to help you answer interview questions.

20. Would I like to work with you on a daily basis?

Of all the things an interviewer looks to answer – once we get past "can you do the job" – this may be the most important one of all. Are you a positive addition to the workplace? Can you carry your fair share of the load?

Do you play well with others? Will you pitch in when needed without grousing? Will you be someone I can trust and rely on?

Qualities you should have to clear the interview

Interviewing is an important part of the hiring process, and it's vital that you make a great impression during a job interview. There are certain skills that will help you succeed during an interview, including communication skills and professionalism. The more you understand about interview skills, the better prepared you'll be for your next interview.

1. Research

Before you go to an interview, it's important to spend time researching both the company and the position you're applying for. There are many ways to research an organization, including:

Reviewing their website, especially the "about" page

Google the company name and read any press releases or other information available

Looking at the company's social media platforms

If possible, talk to the employees of the company

Researching job platforms that provide feedback from current and past employees about the company

You should also take the time to learn as much as you can about the job you are interviewing for. Review the job listing thoroughly, if available, on the company website for the job listing to see if additional details are included and for current employees who are in the same or similar positions.

You can research the job title in general to get a broader idea of the specific duties expected in that position. The more you know about the position, the better prepared you will be when you walk into the interview.

2. Preparation

You should avoid going to the interview unprepared. Doing so can reflect negatively on you as a candidate, and most hiring managers can easily spot applicants who aren't prepared. Set aside at least one hour the day before or the day of the interview for preparation. Here are some actions to take while preparing:

Read the job description again and determine the responsibilities and requirements most relevant to the position.

Come with several specific answers to possible questions related to the position you are applying for and the duties expected of you.

Make a list of essential aspects of the job so that you have it with you when you ask and answer questions during a job interview.

Go over your cover letter and resume you provided to the company so that they remember how you presented yourself in the beginning.

Spend several minutes or even hours researching potential interview questions related to the position you are applying for and the industry the company is a part of.

See less specific interview questions that are not directly related to the job, but may still be asked. For example, practice some behavioral and situational interview questions.

Practice answering interview questions with a friend or family member so that you feel comfortable answering questions during an actual interview.

Prepare several specific examples from your past work experience, including milestones, challenges and successes. These will support your interview answers and help strengthen your responses.

Going into the interview, refer back to the notes you made on the company during the research process to make sure you have fresh information in mind.

3. Punctuality

On the day of interview, make sure that you reach at least 15 minutes before the scheduled interview time. Punctuality is an important attribute that hiring managers and employers value and gives them an idea of how punctual you would be on a daily basis if hired for the position.

To make sure you arrive on time, consider planning and ironing your outfit the night before so it's ready the next day. You should also put your purse or briefcase back the night before and make sure you have a copy of your resume and cover letter on hand. Set an alarm and make sure you have reliable transportation at the time of the interview.

4. Professionalism

There are many aspects that go into professionalism, and they are all important when attending a job interview. To begin with, make sure your attire is professional and tasteful and is neatly pressed and clean.

Avoid wearing clothes that are too casual, too big or small, too revealing or too gaudy. Aim for an outfit with neutral colures that match and aren't distracting or aggressive. If you're unsure of the dress code requirements for an interview, dress more formally to avoid dressing too casually.

When arriving at the interview site, use professional language when checking in and greeting the interviewer. Be polite to everyone you come in contact with, including other staff and the receptionist. The more polite and professional you are in your actions and words, the kinder and more pleasant you will be to employers.

5. Communication Good communication skills are important during the job interview process. This includes written, verbal and nonverbal communication skills. Some important tips to keep in mind when communicating with others during an interview include:

Address the interviewee by name and make sure you pronounce the name or names correctly.

Begin the interview with appropriate small talk. It's best to be prepared with a few conversation starters that are professional and suited for the interview setting.

Match your communication style with the hiring manager. For example, if the hiring manager is communicating in a professional manner, try to match your tone to theirs. If they're more enthusiastic and offer jokes here and there, don't be afraid to do so as long as they're appropriate.

Avoid interrupting the person who is interviewing you.

Do not use jargon or abbreviated language.

Try to avoid using speech fillers like "um" and "like".

Be aware of your nonverbal cues to make sure you are presenting yourself in a professional and positive manner.

6. Listening

Listening skills are another important component of a successful interview experience. It's easy to listen to a person, and while doing so think to yourself about how you would respond. While this may sound wise, it can also prevent you from really catching the person's entire message. Listen carefully and give your full attention to the hiring manager, saying what they have said in your mind or out loud when appropriate, and use nonverbal cues such as these to convey that you are engaged.

You should also ask for clarification if you misunderstood something that was said for communication to be effective. Avoid changing the subject quickly and pay attention to any nonverbal cues the interviewer is giving you, such as facial expressions and tone of voice, to further understand what is being said.

7. Ask Questions

Hiring managers often ask candidates if they have any questions during or after the interview. Interviewers look for candidates who ask genuine questions to help them gain a better understanding of the company and the role. Arrive at the interview prepared with some questions to ask the interviewer that demonstrate genuine interest in the opportunity and provide an opportunity to discuss elements of the job that may not have been covered.

8. Confidence

Confidence has a significant impact on how you are perceived by interviewers. Arrive at the interview prepared to confidently discuss your experience, accomplishments and abilities, expressing your confidence in yourself to perform the duties of the position for which you have applied. Work to exude a balanced and compassionate confidence, rather than just boasting about your abilities.

9. Show interest

It is important to express your genuine interest in the position during a job interview. If you show a sense of disinterest or disinterest, the interviewer may think you don't really want the position or don't care about the outcome of the interview. Work to demonstrate your full interest in the organization and the position and your passion for your work and your ability to perform the job duties.

10. Follow-up

Following up immediately after an interview is considered important by many recruiters and hiring managers. A simple thank you card or thank you email can go a long way to show the interviewer that you are genuinely interested in the position and are grateful for their time. Try sending a follow-up email or note on the day of the interview or the next day at the latest.

11. Show gratitude

No matter how your interview goes, always take a moment to thank the interviewers for their time and consideration. A positive attitude and polite behaviour can go a long way in impressing people.

Remember, the interview is all about you and how well you represent yourself. So be confident and follow the above tips. We are sure you will be able to do a good job!

12. Stay motivated

In case you feel the interview isn't going as well as you hoped, don't be sad or demotivated? Continue to reply honestly and enthusiastically. Remember, a positive attitude can leave a good impression on the interviewer. If you appear sad or disappointed, it shows a lack of ability in handling difficult situations worsening your chances.

13. Do not waste time

The interviewer probably has a very busy day planned. Do not waste their time. Be direct in your answers and do not beat around the bush. There will be some tough questions you may not know the answers to. In such cases, politely accept that you are not aware but ready to learn. Don't try guesswork or try to fool the interviewer. Sometimes tough questions are just a way to see how well you respond under pressure.

14. Know what and when to speak

Keep in mind you are in a formal setting. Even if the interviewer is acting friendly, avoid inappropriate abatements. Don't use casual slang or jargon. In addition, avoid statements about race, religion or politics. Stick to what the interviewer is talking about and respond in a polite and formal manner.

15. Make eye contact

When you talk to an interviewer, be sure to look at them. Don't look down or at the wall or the clock. This shows a lack of confidence. Communicate with the interviewer by making eye contact. This displays confidence while allowing you to make an engaged connection.

16. Be attentive

Good communication skills can go a long way in impressing the interviewer. Listen carefully to everything the interviewer is saying. This is not the time to daydream or be distracted. Match their pace of talking to better connect with them while also making sure you heard what was said

Learn PROFESSIONALS skills

Employees in most roles and industries can grow their careers with professional skills. Professional skills can help you get a new job, advance positions, build workplace relationships and improve your job performance

Professional skills are abilities that can help you be successful at your job. A professional skill describes a habit, personality trait, or ability that positively affects your performance in the workplace. Having these kinds of skills can benefit people in almost all job positions, industries, and work environments.

Professional skills are also called soft skills, meaning skills that can be easily transferred from one job to another. Soft skills refer to how we relate to our environment and the people around us. In contrast, hard skills refer to more technical or specialized knowledge related to a specific job or industry.

Here are details of soft skills that can help further your professional career:

Written and Spoken Communication Skills

Spoken communication skill is related to our body language with tone of voice and written skill is related to write anything by using proper way of grammar, spellings, punctuation, etc.

Developing Written and Spoken Communication Skills will give a chance to get the best job instead of it poor Communication and written skill may result of a negative impact on interviewers. And this can create the problem of misunderstanding, and frustration.

Related Written and Spoken Communication skills include:

Tone

Grammar

Spellings

Use of word as per message

Clarity

Message editing thoroughly

Use of Golden words

Knowing the written and verbal Etiquette

Computer skills

Future in computer field is the brightest future. Whenever you hired for any post in any company then surely you get a computer on your table. You need to know the operating skills of the computer because every company doing their business with the help of computer.

So, the hiring team always check your computer skills while hiring you for the job. Thus, it's most important for you to develop your computer skills for getting a good job as a fresher.

Now if you want to learn any computer course then we are providing the complete training of all Computer Courses for Jobs in our DOTNET Institute through our online mode. You can download our online mobile app as we are providing all courses in our online mobile app.

Related Computer skills include:

Office Automation

Microsoft Word

Microsoft Excel

Google

Internet

Using Drives

Be Responsible

Be responsible means you are able to be trusted to do what is right or, having care for something as per requirement and trust. There are many responsibilities to run a company or business. And the owner always like the employees those take over the maximum responsibilities.

You can get the best increment and promotion by becoming the responsible person in your job. The company owner's always provide the best thing for the responsible employees.

Related Be Responsible skills include:

Courage to act

Self-Trust

Make Deadlines

Supportive

Creative

Adaptability

Work Flexibility
skill is Be Responsible

Leadership skills

Leadership skills help you encourage and organize other people to reach a shared goal. Whether you're a manager, project leader or team member, these skills allow you to motivate others. Leadership is not just one skill but a combination of several different skills.

If you're applying for jobs that require you to take the initiative and be a leader—whether as a manager or among your peers—you should list leadership skills on your resume. If you aren't sure how to highlight your leadership skills on your resume, you can get professional

Top 10 Leadership Skills

Almost any positive soft skill can be considered a leadership skill. For example, active listening helps leaders complete projects by listening to their team's ideas and concerns. Empathy helps leaders understand how their team feels about their workload or workplace relationships.

Here is a list of valuable leadership skills for anyone applying for work or looking to advance in their career:

1. Decisiveness

The ability to make decisions is a valuable leadership skill that can help move projects along faster and improve efficiency. Strong decision-making skills aid your ability to choose solutions to challenges. Effective decisiveness requires research, evaluation, problem-solving and goal-setting, often with quick turnaround times. Decision makers draw from their own experience with similar tasks, evaluate what might work best, make decisions and be confident in taking responsibility for the outcome.

2. Honesty

Integrity is often seen simply as truthfulness or honesty. However, it also means having a set of strong values and standing by them. It's behaving respectfully, even when no one is looking. Integrity in the workplace often means making ethical choices and helping the company maintain a positive image. All businesses want to hire employees who have a strong sense of integrity.

3. Creativity

Good leaders often have to make decisions that don't have clear answers, requiring them to think out of the box. Creative leaders foster the free exchange of new ideas. They inspire innovation and collaboration in the workplace. A leader with creativity also shows the following skills:

4. Flexibility

A good leader must be flexible, accepting last minute changes or new issues. You should also be open to suggestions and feedback. Managing the unexpected, initiating new courses of action and proposing new solutions can have a positive impact on your team. Resilient leaders display skills such as:

5. Positive Attitude

An effective leader knows that a positive attitude can go a long way in the workplace. You work to create a positive work environment even during stressful periods. Employees are more likely to be productive and motivated to do their best when they are happy and feel valued. Skills that can help foster a good work environment include:

6. Communication

Good leaders can clearly explain things from organizational goals to specific tasks. Open communication between executives, managers and team members fosters a seamless environment and transparency. A good leader needs a variety of communication skills, including:

7. Relationship-building

Leadership requires building and maintaining a strong, collaborative team of individuals working toward the same goal. Relationship-building, also known as team building, requires effective communication skills and other leadership strengths such as conflict resolution. Once you understand each other, you can benefit from assessing strengths, delegating tasks, and meeting your goals more seamlessly. A successful leader who is good at building relationships will also have the following skills:

8.problem-solving

Good leaders are skilled at problem-solving issues that arise on the job. Effective problem-solving often requires staying calm and identifying a step-by-step solution. Problem-solving skills can help leaders make quick decisions, resolve obstacles with their team and external teams alike, and ensure projects are finished on time, according to the specifications. Leaders who are effective problem-solvers also have the following skills:

9.dependency

Being a trustworthy leader means that people can trust and rely on you. A dependable person follows through on plans and keeps promises. Strong relationships built by a responsible leader create a resilient team that can work through difficulties as they arise. Being a dependable professional means meeting deadlines, being straightforward, meeting obligations or communicating quickly when you can't meet a promise or goal, and having a backup plan. Confident leaders also have the following skills:

10. Ability to teach and mentor

One skill that sets leadership apart from many other competencies is the ability to teach and mentor. Helps organizations scale by giving direct reports the opportunity to effectively teach associates or grow in their careers. Often, this skill requires leaders to think less about themselves and more about helping their team succeed. To be successful as a leader teaching and mentoring a team, you can hone the following related skills:

CHAPTER EIGHT

Team work

People who work well on teams have interpersonal skills that help them collaborate effectively. Many employees work in groups with their co-workers or supervisors to fulfil at least some of their job responsibilities. Professionals with teamwork skills understand how to complete their tasks while remaining aware of the assignments and needs of others.

The skills needed to excel in teamwork include:

help

Reliability

desire to help others

friendship

ability to persuade or persuade others

Recognition

Tolerance

working for a common goal

help

Emotional Intelligence

Emotional intelligence refers to how we express our feelings, relate to others, and interpret others' behavior. Professionals with emotional intelligence can sense how others are feeling through their actions, speech, or behavior. If you have emotional intelligence, you can also identify, evaluate, and assess your feelings. Emotional intelligence helps professionals in many social settings, whether with clients, co-workers, or managers.

Here are some skills to develop if you want to improve your emotional intelligence:

self-awareness

sympathy

initiative

Conscientiousness, or the willingness and ability to treat others well
self-regulation
Reliability
Sympathy

Organization

Organizational abilities help you complete projects and duties. Professionals with organization skills understand how to prioritize tasks, make plans and implement solutions. A person's time management is often closely related to their organizational abilities as many employers require them to efficiently complete projects according to their deadlines.

The skills needed to excel in an organization include:
stress management
making plans
delegation
attention to details
Punctuality
executive functioning, such as prioritizing duties
time management
distribution of resources
dependency

Flexibility

Supervisors often appreciate employees who can adapt to a variety of situations and challenges. Flexible professionals can understand different points of view, seek alternative solutions to problems, and change their job responsibilities or processes as needed.

To become more resilient, consider strengthening these skills:
staying calm in stressful situations
adaptability
receptivity
face challenges with a positive attitude
proactiveness
critical thinking
Patience
Willingness to consider additional information or change your opinion
Intuition

self-motivation

Self-motivated professional takes initiative. If you are self-motivated, you generally require minimal supervision to begin or complete your duties.

Many supervisors appreciate employees who complete tasks and work hard regardless of their supervision level.

To work on your self-motivation, consider developing these skills:

self-starter

Independence

desire to achieve

resilience

commitment to goals

optimism

initiative

ambition

willingness to grow and change

Openness to learn

Professionals willing to learn new information and skills may receive more attention from hiring managers. Most jobs, industries or companies change over time, so employers appreciate candidates who are receptive to learning new concepts, capabilities or processes.

To show your willingness to learn, focus on developing these abilities:

receptive to constructive criticism

Excitement

openness to personal growth

initiative

learning agility, or the ability to develop new skills

self-motivation

Continuous engagement with industry, local, global or other news

Tips for Developing Professional Skills

Here are some tips to help you practice and improve your professional abilities:

observe other professionals

Pay attention to how team members, supervisors, distributors, and others behave in their work environment. See how the professionals around you interact with each other, accomplish their tasks, and navigate workplace processes. If you find a co-worker who has a soft skill you'd like to develop, try to emulate some of their behaviour or attitude.

Attend conferences and workshops

Conferences, workshops, and related events allow you to practice your professional skills outside of the workplace. Focus on communicating effectively, listening actively, and other soft skills while networking with other professionals.

Lectures, workshops, conferences and other professional events sometimes choose soft skills as their themes. For example, you might find a webinar that discusses the role of confidence in the workplace. Seeking out events like this can help further develop your professional skills.

resolve workplace conflicts

Although you may have conflicts with your co-workers at times, try to resolve these conflicts collaboratively. Managers and team members alike prefer to collaborate with an employee they know can continue to act, strategize, and communicate politely but clearly during challenging situations. Try to view conflicts as opportunities to learn more about how you and your co-workers can effectively collaborate, problem solve and work as a team.

Ask questions

Ask people more questions during interactions. People who ask questions more frequently than argue or assert their own opinions may excel at many soft skills, such as communication, open-mindedness or willingness to learn. You can ask someone questions about the subject even if you know a lot about it or have a different opinion. Focusing on asking questions can help you gain insights into new perspectives or areas within the subject. If you decide at a later date to debate or offer your own opinion on the subject, you'll then be able to provide a more complex or thorough perspective.

be receptive to feedback

Work on being open to constructive feedback. Many desired professional skills are related to a person's ability to listen to, evaluate, and apply an assessment of someone else's work or performance. Even if you don't agree with the response, consider what the other person said before dismissing or arguing. Evaluating the feedback other people give you as objectively as possible can help you figure out how to rationally discuss feedback and determine which parts of it to incorporate into your habits.

build positive relationships

Develop positive relationships with your co-workers, customers, managers, and other professionals with whom you work. Many professional skills describe your behaviour, habits, and communication methods when interacting with others. You may find it easier to have cooperative and friendly interactions if you already have positive relationships in the workplace.

For example, you can try to have real conversations with your co-workers and customers. Ask about their weekend plans, hobbies, pets, and other workplace-appropriate topics that can give you more insight into their personal lives. You can also discuss your interests and plans, as this can help people feel more comfortable talking about you.

practice self-care

Developing new skills is usually easier when you're already meeting your basic needs. Take care of yourself by eating nutritious foods, spending time with loved ones, getting enough sleep, and making time for activities you enjoy. A healthy mind and body can help you learn and adapt to new habits.

CHAPTER NINE

The Importance of a Resume

The resume acts as a bridge between you and the prospective recruiter. Hence the importance of a resume can never be underestimated. So, to make the first impression, it is imperative that your resume stands out from the crowd first. It is up to you how do you want to be remembered by the hiring manager, Since companies do not have that much amount of time to interview each and every candidate, they require resumes from candidates to select the best ones to work with them.

Rejection happens, and it goes on and on until they find something interesting in one particular resume. This is the time when a well-structured, clean and precise resume plays its part. You might be thinking why is it so important to have a resume? Let's find out:

Resume reaches the recruiter's table much before than you do: Yes, before you reach recruiter's office, your resume does so. Generally, every company asks for your resume first, they go through the work that you have done so far and if it matches their requirement, thumbs up! So, a well-written resume does half of the work for you here only. Hence it is very much important to have a structured and concise resume to make the first impression work for you.

Resume tells about you: A resume speaks a great deal about you as a professional. It says what you have done in the past. What are you doing currently and where exactly you are heading towards?

Just imagine a small piece of paper talks so much about you including past, present, and future. Doesn't that sound amazing? But remember this story of past, present and future needs to be conveyed quickly, else they will lose interest. So, this job of telling a short story can be little tricky. Hence you might need help in drafting your resume by professionals.

To convince that you are the one: You must be thinking that it is easy for you to convince the recruiter that you are the most suitable candidate for the vacant position. But that will only be possible when you are there for face-to-face round. Before you appear for the face-to-face interview, your resume would convince them first that you are the most eligible candidate for the position offered or not. Now you must have understood what important role does a resume play for you.

To sell your skills: Through a well-written resume, you can sell the skills which you have accumulated over these years. You can let the recruiter know what all skills that you have acquired through different jobs and how you are going to utilize them for the betterment of the prospective organization. This is exactly what recruiter need to know now-a-days. They want to know in which way your skills will prove beneficial for their organization. And if your resume is successful in telling them so, the purpose is served.

To grab an interview: Unless and until your dad or a very close relative owns a company, where you can easily join without much ado, you are surely going to need a good resume. And ultimately the purpose of the resume is to get an interview. And writing a resume is the first step towards that direction. So, do not ignore the importance of writing a good resume.

To Brand Yourself: It is very essential to create your own brand in this professional world and this journey starts right after your college and studies. When you enter a professional world to work, it is essential that from the very first day you have to set things right. To showcase your knowledge, your skills, experience, expertise, and accomplishments, it is necessary to have a perfectly written resume which can portray you as a good professional or a budding professional who is ready to face this challenging world.

Quick but lasting first impression: You must have heard of the saying that the first impression is the last impression. It goes well with the resume as well. In the bulk of the resumes, if one resume stands out and it gives a feeling that yes, this is the one, then working hard on your resume is worth it. The recruiter would likely ignore the resume which is text heavy and difficult to read. So, you now get the point what your resume should NOT look like. Try to keep it simple, easy to read and easy to understand.

Summarize your career aspiration: A good resume recapitulates your career so well that recruiters do not need to put in the hard effort just to scan and go through your resume in details to understand your profile. So, make sure that the summary section of your resume is robust enough to give a good glimpse of your whole career in short.

For those who have no work experience so far and applying as a fresher, it is suggested that they talk about their projects, internships, industrial visits, trainings and additional value-added course in the summary section, so that even if a recruiter chooses not to go through the entire detailed resume, at least the summary section will be good enough for him to understand and gauge your worth as a candidate.

To show your achievements: You cannot wait for the recruiter to call you to know about your career history and accomplishments so far. That sound something like you have not written and posted the letter to your friend, and you are expecting him/her to understand your feeling/situation. So, it is imperative to write a good resume to showcase your achievements to tell your success story so far.

Just resume: While looking for a job, it is essential to have a good resume but make sure it is just the resume. Do not make it so fancy or full of jargons to make it cumbersome for a recruiter to read. And also, one thing you need to keep in mind that when you are sending your resume to a recruiter, send the resume only or at the most attach the cover letter. Do not include or attach a letter of recommendations, copies of your education mark sheet, reference letter or anything else unless this is asked for.

You are sure of your work: Many a time it happens that we plan and execute something, even be successful in our endeavour, but after sometime, may be a year or so, we tend to forget those. We see the current challenges and try to cope up with them.

So, if you have a good resume, you will remember each and everything you have done and achieved in your professional career. It will happen if you keep updating your resume whenever you change a job and join a new company, whenever you get a new role, a new project, a new team to handle.

Take a note when the company is rewarding you for your work. That does not mean that you make your resume, a daily diary, just keep note of the important happenings in your professional front. And you can always edit your resume keeping the master copy with you. And remember even the greatest writer in the literary world need the help of the editor. You can read it, re-read it, proofread it ten times, but it is always good to take a second opinion

CHAPTER TEN

Make a best Resume that will show your knowledge and skills

Your resume is the most important tool in your job-seeking arsenal. A good resume can help you get your foot in the door, while a bad resume will likely keep you from even being considered.

This resume guide will teach you, step-by-step, how to make a resume that will help you stand out from the crowd. We'll provide tips on how to format your resume, what information to include, and how to tailor your resume for different jobs using the right keywords.

Step 1. Choose a resume format

The right resume format can help highlight your strengths and downplay your weaknesses. It can also make it easier for recruiters to scan your resume and identify the key information they are looking for.

There are three standard resume formats to choose from.

Chronological Resume

This is the most popular resume format, especially for job seekers with lots of relevant experience. This format lists your work history in reverse chronological order, with your most recent jobs listed first. It's ideal for:

Job seekers with a lot of professional work experience.

People with no employment gaps.

Those who want to showcase their career progression over time.

Functional Resume (also known as a Skills-Based Resume)

The functional resume is organized around your transferable skills and abilities rather than your work history. It helps you downplay your lack of experience in a particular field. While it is helpful for certain situations, it's not always the best. Recruiters sometimes don't like the functional resume format because it can make it seem like you're trying to conceal something. So be wary of that.

Under each skill you list, try to add bullet points that provide specific examples of times when you've used that skill. This format is ideal for:

Recent graduates

Entry-level job seekers

Career changers

Those with gaps in their employment history

Hybrid Resume (also known as a Combination Resume)

A hybrid resume can be a great way to showcase both your work history and your skills. For many job seekers, it's the best resume format. With this format, you would begin with a brief overview of your skills and accomplishments, followed by a chronological listing of your employment history. This format is ideal for:

Mid-level job seekers with some experience in their field.

Career changers who need to highlight transferable skills.

People re-entering the workforce.

Step 2. Add your contact information and personal details

This is one of the most important sections of your resume. If hiring managers can't contact you, it doesn't matter how great the rest of your resume is. So, you need to make sure that your contact info is accurate and up-to-date.

The following information should appear at the top of your resume:

Name

Phone number

Location (City, State, Zip Code)

Email Address

LinkedIn profile URL

Step 3. Write a standout resume headline

One way to make sure your resume stands out is to write a catchy headline. This is a concise, one-line description of who you are as a candidate.

A well-written headline can grab a recruiter's attention and encourage them to take a more detailed look at your resume. It can also highlight your most relevant skills and experience, making it easier for recruiters to see why you would be a good fit for the role.

You should place your headline near the top of your resume, so it's one of the first things that a hiring manager or recruiter sees.

Resume headlines are most beneficial for people who have a lot of relevant experience, but anyone can use them.

If you don't have any experience or are applying for an entry-level job, you can use your resume headline to show off your soft skills, your proficiency with tools, or your winning personal attributes.

When writing your headline, it's crucial to include the job title that appears at the top of the description of the job you're applying for. This is the most impactful keyword of all, and the headline is a good place to put it, especially if you haven't held the exact position before.

Step 4. Add your resume summary statement or resume objective

Most recruiters only spend between six and eight seconds looking at a resume before they make a decision about a job candidate, according to a study by Ladders.

This means you need to make a strong first impression! You can do this by adding a resume summary statement underneath your resume headline.

A summary statement is a brief paragraph or a set of bullet points that summarizes your professional qualifications.

Your summary statement should expand on your resume headline and provide evidence of your skills, achievements, and experience.

Resume summaries are ideal for job seekers who have plenty of relevant work experience and accomplishments that can be tied to actual numbers.

If you don't have much job experience or are changing careers, you could write a resume objective statement instead.

Your resume objective basically explains what the object of your resume is. It is a short statement that communicates your reason for wanting to work in a new field. It should include:

The job title or field you are interested in.

Any transferable skills that make you a good fit for the position.

Relevant accomplishments that demonstrate how you would excel in the new role.

Your career goals and how the position you are applying for can help you achieve them.

For example, if you are a recent college graduate seeking a position in marketing, your resume objective might state: "To secure a position in marketing where I can utilize my creativity and analytical skills to contribute to the company's success."

Step 5. Add keywords and skills that are ATS-friendly

Before you move on to the next step, it's important to determine what keywords and skills you need to have on your resume.

Why? Because when you submit your resume, it most likely won't go to a live human being – it will go straight into a computer database.

Employers receive hundreds and even thousands of resumes for every job opening. They don't have time to look at all of them.

To solve this problem, many employers now use application tracking systems (ATS) to automatically collect, review, and sort resumes. In fact, 99 percent of Fortune 500 companies now use ATS to help them manage the hiring process.

Having the right keywords on your resume is important because hiring managers use keywords to search through their ATS database for the best job candidates.

These keywords are usually job titles or specific skills. If your resume doesn't contain the keywords hiring managers are searching for, it will sit in the database, unseen.

This is why it's crucial to include keywords on your resume that are relevant to the job you are applying for. But how do you know which keywords to use?

Just look at the job description. Take note of the skills and keywords that appear the most. Then add these skills and keywords to your resume when appropriate.

To get the best results, tailor each and every resume you create to the specific job you're applying for — your resume is not a one-size-fits-all document!

Step 6. Detail your work experience

Now it's time to get to the heart of your resume – the "work experience" section. This is the section employers will spend the most time looking at when they consider your resume.

If you get this part right, you'll be well on your way to creating a strong resume that will land you plenty of job interviews!

The first things a recruiter looks at on your resume are the job titles you've held and the companies you've worked with. Make this information easy to find by listing each job in reverse-chronological order (latest job first).

Each job should have its own subheading that includes the following information:

Company name and location – Include the full name of the company you worked for followed by the city and state of its location.

Job title – Be as specific as possible to ensure that employers know exactly what your role was within the company.

Start and end dates – Include the month and year for each position. If you only list the year, it may appear as though you are omitting information.

Achievements and responsibilities – These can be listed using bullet points. Include hard numbers and metrics wherever possible.

Our research has found that this sequence offers maximum applicant tracking system (ATS) compatibility.

CHAPTER ELEVEN

Tips for the resume

I am also sharing some tips for the resume read it.

Tip #1: Highlight achievements as well as responsibilities

One of the biggest mistakes people make when writing a resume is only listing their job responsibilities. These are tasks that you're expected to perform as part of your job. They can include things like:

Answering customer questions and complaints

Scheduling and coordinating appointments

Taking inventory and ordering supplies

Maintaining records and filing paperwork

Training new employees

Listing your job responsibilities gives a potential employer an idea of what you did day-to-day, but it doesn't reveal how well you did it.

That's why it's important to highlight your specific accomplishments in prior roles.

For example, if you increased sales, reduced costs, or implemented new processes or technologies, be sure to mention these accomplishments.

Instead of writing "managed a team of 12 people," write "managed a team of 12 people, consistently meeting or exceeding quarterly targets."

This not only demonstrates that you are an asset to any organization, but it gives employers confidence that you're capable of handling the job.

Here's an example of a resume that does a good job of listing both responsibilities and accomplishments:

Not every career lends itself to easily-quantifiable achievements. For example, someone who works in a warehouse might have responsibilities that include stocking shelves, unloading trucks, and packaging items for shipment.

While these responsibilities might not seem like much, they're actually essential for keeping the warehouse running smoothly. The ability to work efficiently and effectively is a valuable skill in any field.

So, next time you're feeling like you don't have anything to list as an accomplishment, take a step back and look at the bigger picture. Chances are, you've achieved more than you realize!

Tip #2: Use action verbs

Action verbs are key when it comes to writing an engaging and compelling resume. They help paint a clearer picture of your qualifications and increase the overall impact of your resume.

Instead of simply stating that you were "responsible for" a certain task or project, explain how you took charge and made it happen. For example, you could say that you "spearheaded" a new initiative or "coordinated" a complex team effort.

By using powerful verbs, you'll not only make your resume more interesting to read, but you'll also demonstrate the kind of can-do attitude that employers are looking for.

Tip #3: Use active voice, not passive

Always try to use an active voice instead of a passive voice when writing your resume.

In an active voice, the subject of the sentence is doing the verb. For example, "The cashier counted the money." In a passive voice, the subject is being acted upon by the verb. For example, "The money was counted by the cashier."

Active voice is preferred over passive voice because it's more direct, concise, easier to read, and it makes you sound more confident and authoritative.

When used with an action verb, an active voice can subconsciously influence a recruiter into thinking that the applicant is competent and capable. For example, "managed a team of 12" is more powerful than "was responsible for a team of 12."

Tip #4: Use numbers

One of the best ways to make your resume stand out is to use numbers. In fact, job seekers who use numbers in their resumes increase their hire ability by 40%, according to a study by Talent Works.

Whenever possible, quantify your achievements with numbers that illustrate the scope of your work. For example, instead of saying "created marketing campaigns," you could write "created 10 successful marketing campaigns that generated a 20% increase in leads."

By using numbers, you give hiring managers a better sense of your value, making it more likely that you'll land the job you want.

Here are some more examples of using numbers (with action verbs underlined):

Saved $7 million while introducing nationwide transport service for medical patients.

Generated a utility income increase of 45% within 2 months by designing and deploying an enhanced bill back process.

Achieved 150% sales growth by leading a multifunctional team to define, refine, and roll-out a cross-channel, ten-year brand strategy.

Finally, If you have gaps in your employment history, be prepared to explain them in a cover letter or during an interview.

However, don't let a few months or years off work deter you from applying for a position – focus on highlighting your skills and strengths, and let your work experience speak for itself.

Step 7. Showcase your skills

When writing your resume, be sure to include a skills section. This is the perfect place to mention all the skills and know-how that make you the ideal candidate for the job.

Pay particular attention to the skills that are listed in the job description of the position you are applying for. As we've seen, including these keywords on your resume greatly increases the chance that your resume will be seen by an actual hiring manager, leading to a job interview.

There are two types of skills you can include in your skills section: hard skills and soft skills.

Hard skills are the specific skills and knowledge that you need to perform a certain task or job. They are usually quantifiable and easy to measure. Examples of hard skills include:

Computer programming

Copywriting

Data analysis

Programming

Accounting

Graphic design

Web development

SEO

Soft skills, on the other hand, are interpersonal skills that help you interact with others. They are more difficult to quantify but are just as important in the workplace. Examples of soft skills include:

Communication

Leadership

Teamwork

Problem solving

Time management

Self-management

Critical thinking

Flexibility

Soft skills are important because they're transferable. This means they can be applied to any number of settings and can help you succeed in any type of job.

Also, unlike hard skills, which can become outdated quickly, soft skills are always in demand. As the world changes and technology advances, soft skills will become even more important.

Here's an example of a skills section for a mechanical engineer that includes both hard and soft skills:

Step 8. Add your education and certifications

You need to include your education somewhere on your resume, but where it appears depends on your individual circumstances.

If you are just starting out in your career, it's generally a good idea to include your education section near the top of your resume. Recent grads can include relevant coursework, societies, organizations, and extracurriculars that strengthen their candidacy.

However, if you are a few years into your career, your education can appear at the bottom of your resume. This is because your work experience will be more relevant to potential employers at this point in your career.

Unless you're applying to a job that puts extra emphasis on education (like academia, law, or medicine), most job seekers can get away with providing only the following information on their resume:

Name of school

School location

Degree

Year graduated

If you have earned any professional certifications that are relevant to the job you are applying for, then you should definitely include them on your resume.

You can list your certifications right under your education information. Be sure to include the name of the certification, the issuing authority, and the date of certification. If the certification is still valid, you can also mention that.

If you have earned multiple certifications, then you can list them in order of importance, with the most relevant ones appearing first.

Here's an example of what the education section looks like on a pharmacist's resume:

Step 9. Additional resume sections (optional)

Your resume is your opportunity to shine. It's your chance to show potential employers who you are and what you're capable of.

One way to really stand out is to include additional information that showcases your skills and accomplishments. If applicable, consider adding the following resume sections:

Languages

In today's global economy, knowing foreign languages can give you a competitive edge over other candidates. Many businesses are looking for employees who can communicate with customers and clients in their native language.

On your resume, list the languages you speak in order of proficiency, starting with your strongest language. Also, specify whether you are fluent, proficient, or conversational in each language. For example:

Fluent in Spanish and English

Proficient in French and conversational in German

Conversational in Japanese

Hobbies and interests

Many people believe that hobbies should remain separate from their professional lives. However, including information about your hobbies on a resume can actually give employers a better sense of who you are as a person.

For example, if you enjoy hiking, it shows that you are physically active and have a sense of adventure. If you enjoy cooking, it shows that you are creative and have a keen interest in food.

When listing your hobbies, make sure to keep it short and sweet. You don't need to go into great detail about every single hobby you have. Just mention a few that you think are relevant and leave it at that.

Publications

If you have been published in any capacity, it is generally a good idea to include this information on your resume, especially if it's relevant to the job you're applying to. Most employers love to see that you can communicate effectively in writing.

If you're not sure where to start, list any published articles, blog posts, books, or even whitepapers that you have written. Be sure to include the title, publisher, and date. For example:

"The Impact of Social Media on Businesses." The Journal of Business, December 2021.

Awards

If you have won any awards that are relevant to the job you're applying to, you should absolutely include them on your resume. Awards will impress potential employers and help you to stand out from the competition.

Be sure to list the name of the award, the date you received it, and a brief description of the award. For example:

"Top Salesperson" (January 2020) – Awarded to the salesperson with the highest sales numbers for the month.

Volunteer experience

If you have any volunteer experience, don't forget to add it to your resume!

According to a LinkedIn survey, 20% of employers say they have hired a candidate because of their volunteer experience. The survey also showed that job seekers who volunteer are 27% more likely to be hired than non-volunteers.

When adding your volunteer experience to your resume, list the name of the organization, the dates of your service, and a brief description of your duties and responsibilities. For example:

Woodstock Food Bank, Jan 2019-present

Led a team of 10 volunteers in sorting and distributing donated items to local families in need.

Organized monthly food drives that collected an average of 500 lbs of food per month.

Personal projects

Many professionals use their skills outside of the office. In fact, 57 million workers participate in the gig economy in the US.

Adding your side projects to your resume can be a great way to demonstrate your commitment to lifelong learning and professional development.

Examples of personal projects include designing websites, creating a YouTube channel, coding apps, writing a book, running an ecommerce store, consulting, or starting any kind of new business.

When choosing personal projects to include on your resume, be sure to select those that are most relevant to the position you are applying for.

Step 10. Format your resume so it can be easily read by an ATS

Formatting your resume correctly is absolutely vital if you want to get more job interviews.

Why? Because your resume most likely will go straight into a computer database (ATS) after you submit it. If your resume can't be read by the ATS due to formatting issues, then all your hard work will be for nothing.

So, pay close attention to these formatting dos and don'ts!

Step 11. Add a cover letter

When you submit your resume, you'll most likely also have to submit a cover letter.

Think of a cover letter as a quick preview of your skills and experience. The goal is to make the hiring manager interested in you so they will want to learn more.

The best cover letters are usually one page long so the message is clear and easy to understand.

How to Write a Cover Letter

Contact Information – Include your full name, address (including zip code), and phone number with area code. Your contact information should be in the upper left corner of your cover letter.

Greeting – Ideally, you should find out the name of the hiring manager and greet them directly. You can usually find the hiring manager's name by searching the company website or even calling the company and asking which hiring manager is assigned to this particular position.

Opening – Think of your opening sentence as your chance to grab the hiring manager's attention and get them excited to learn more about you. What can you do that nobody else can?

Body – You need to sell yourself in this section. The best way to do this is by providing examples of your measurable accomplishments. These are powerful because they show tangible proof of your abilities. Only include the most relevant and positive information about yourself in your cover letter.

Closing – This section is used to thank the hiring manager for their time and to point out any attachments (website, portfolio, samples). Be professional and don't sound too eager, or you might sound desperate.

Use Keywords – If you can, use some of the same keywords from the job description in your cover letter. This will show employers that you have read through the job description carefully and that you understand what they are looking for in a candidate.

A great cover letter can make all the difference when applying to a job. It allows employers to see beyond your resume and get an idea of who you are as a person—and if you would be a good fit for their company culture.

By following these tips, you can write a great cover letter that will improve your chances of getting an interview!

And last but not least...

Remember to thoroughly proofread your resume and cover letter!

Proofreading is one of the most important things you can do before sending off your application. A single typo or mistake can make you look unprofessional and could cost you the job.

If you don't think your proofreading skills are good enough, ask a friend or family member to help you out. You can also use a free online proofreading tool like Grammarly.

Remember, sending your resume off without carefully proofreading it could spell disaster. So be sure to take the time to update your resume and review it for typos and errors. It could make all the difference in whether or not you get a job interview.

CHAPTER TWELVE

Important Question and answers for the Interview

Wouldn't it be great if you knew exactly what questions a hiring manager would be asking you in your next job interview?

We can't read minds, unfortunately, but we'll give you the next best thing: a list of 50 of the most commonly asked interview questions, along with advice for answering them all.

While we don't recommend having a canned response for every interview question (in fact, please don't), we do recommend spending some time getting comfortable with what you might be asked, what hiring managers are really looking for in your responses, and what it takes to show that you're the right person for the job.

Consider this list your interview question and answer study guide. (And don't miss our bonus list at the end, with links out to resources on specific types of interview questions—about emotional intelligence or diversity and inclusion, for example—and interview questions by role, from accountant to project manager to teacher.

Tell me about yourself.

This question seems simple, so many people fail to prepare for it, but it's crucial. Here's the deal: Don't give your complete employment (or personal) history. Instead, give a pitch—one that's concise and compelling and that shows exactly why you're the right fit for the job. Muse writer and MIT career counsellor Lily Zhang recommends using a present, past, future formula. Talk a little bit about your current role (including the scope and perhaps one big accomplishment), then give some background as to how you got there and experience you have that's relevant. Finally, segue into why you want—and would be perfect for—this role.

Possible answer to "Tell me about yourself."

"Well, I'm currently an account executive at Smith, where I handle our top-performing client. Before that, I worked at an agency where I was on three different major national healthcare brands. And while I really enjoyed the work that I did, I'd love the chance to dig in much deeper with one specific healthcare company, which is why I'm so excited about this opportunity with Metro Health Centre."

Walk me through your resume.

Like "Tell me about yourself," this question is a common interview opener. But instead of framing your answer around what qualities and skills make you best for the position, your answer should group your qualifications by your past jobs and tell your career story. You might choose to tell this story chronologically, especially if there's a great anecdote about what set you on this path. Or, as with "Tell me about yourself," you can begin with your present job then talk about what brought you here and where you're going next. But regardless, when you speak about your "past" and "present," highlight your most relevant experiences and accomplishments for this job and wrap up by talking about the future, i.e., connect your past and present together to show why this job should be the next one you add to your resume.

"Well, as you can see from my resume, I took a bit of a winding road to get to where I am today. In college, I double majored in chemistry and communications. I found early on that working in a lab all day wasn't for me and at some point, I realized I looked forward to the lab class I TA'ed the most.

"So, when I graduated, I found a job in sales for a consumer healthcare products company, where I drew on my teaching experience and learned even more about tailoring your message and explaining complex health concepts to people without a science background. Then, I moved into a sales training role at a massive company where I was responsible for teaching recent graduates the basics of selling. My trainees on average had more deals closed in their first quarter than any of the other trainers' cohorts. Plus, I got so much satisfaction from finding the right way to train each new hire and watching them progress and succeed. It reminded me of my time as a TA in college. That's when I started taking night classes to earn my chemistry teaching certificate.

"I left my full-time job last year to complete my student teaching at P.S. 118 in Manhattan, and over the summer, I worked for a science camp, teaching kids from the ages of 10 to 12 about basic chemistry concepts and best practices for safe experiments. Now, I'm excited to find my first full-time teaching job, and your district is my top choice. The low student-to-teacher ratio will let me take the time to teach each student in the best way for them—which is my favourite part of the job."

How did you hear about this position?

Another seemingly innocuous interview question, this is actually a perfect opportunity to stand out and show your passion for and connection to the company. For example, if you found out about the gig through a friend or professional contact, name-drop that person, then share why you were so excited about the job. If you discovered the company through an event or article, share that. Even if you found the listing through a random job board, share what, specifically, caught your eye about the role.

Possible answer to "How did you hear about this position?"

"I heard about an opening on the product team through a friend of a friend, Akiko, and since I'm a big fan of your work and have been following you for a while I decided it would be a great role for me to apply for."

Why do you want to work at this company?

Beware of generic answers! If what you say can apply to a whole slew of other companies, or if your response makes you sound like every other candidate, you're missing an opportunity to stand out. Zhang recommends one of four strategies: Do your research and point to something that makes the company unique that really appeals to you; talk about how you've watched the company grow and change since you first heard of it; focus on the organization's opportunities for future growth and how you can contribute to it; or share what's gotten you excited from your interactions with employees so far. Whichever route you choose, make sure to be specific. And if you can't figure out why you'd want to work at the company you're interviewing with by the time you're well into the hiring process? It might be a red flag telling you that this position is not the right fit.

Possible answer to "Why do you want to work at this company?"

"I saw on The Muse that you were also hiring for new positions on the West Coast to support your new operations there. I did some more reading about the new data center you're building there and that excites me as I know this means there'll be opportunities to train new teammates. I also learned through a Wall Street Journal article that you're expanding in Mexico as well. I speak Spanish fluently and would be eager to step up and help liaise whenever necessary."

Why do you want this job?

Again, companies want to hire people who are passionate about the job, so you should have a great answer about why you want the position. (And if you don't? You probably should apply elsewhere.) First, identify a couple of key factors that make the role a great fit for you (e.g., "I love customer support because I love the constant human interaction and the satisfaction that comes from helping someone solve a problem"), then share why you love the company (e.g., "I've always been passionate about education, and I think you're doing great things, so I want to be a part of it").

Possible answer to "Why do you want this job?"

"I've always been a fan of X Co's products and I've spent countless hours playing your games. I know that your focus on unique stories is what drew me and other fans into your games initially and keeps us coming back for more. I've followed X Co on social media for a while, and I've always loved how you have people in different departments interact with users. So I was psyched when I came across this posting for a social media manager with TikTok experience. At my last job, I was responsible for launching our TikTok account and growing it to 10,000 followers in six months. Between that experience, my love of gaming, and my deep knowledge of your games and fanbase, I know I could make this TikTok account something special and exciting.

Why should we hire you?

This interview question seems forward (not to mention intimidating!), but if you're asked it, you're in luck: There's no better setup for you to sell yourself and your skills to the hiring manager. Your job here is to craft an answer that covers three things: that you can not only do the work, but also deliver great results; that you'll really fit in with the team and culture; and that you'd be a better hire than any of the other candidates.

Possible answer to "Why should we hire you?"

"I know it's been an exciting time for General Tech—growing so much and acquiring several start-ups—but I also know from experience that it can be challenging for the sales team to understand how new products fit in with the existing ones. It's always easier to sell the product you know, so the newer stuff can get short-changed, which can have company-wide ramifications. I have over a decade of experience as a sales trainer, but more importantly, most of those years were working with sales teams that were in the exact same boat Gen Tech is in now. Growth is wonderful, but only if the rest of the company can keep up. I'm confident I can make sure your sales team is confident and enthusiastic about selling new products by implementing an ongoing sales training curriculum that emphasizes where they sit in a product line-up."

What can you bring to the company?

When interviewers ask this question, they don't just want to hear about your background. They want to see that you understand what problems and challenges they're facing as a company or department as well as how you'll fit into the existing organization. Read the job description closely, do your research on the company, and make sure you pay attention in your early round interviews to understand any issues you're being hired to solve. Then, the key is to connect your skills and experiences to what the company needs and share an example that shows how you've done similar or transferable work in the past.

Possible answer to "What can you bring to the company?"

"As Jocelyn talked about in our interview earlier, Pepco is looking to expand its market to small business owners with less than 25 employees, so I'd bring my expertise in this area and my experience in guiding a sales team that's selling to these customers for the first time. In most of my past roles, this segment has been my focus and in my current role, I also played a big part in creating our sales strategies when the business began selling to these customers. I worked with my managers to develop the sales script. I also listened in on a number of sales calls with other account execs who were selling to these customers for the first time and gave them pointers and other feedback. In the first quarter, our 10-person sales team closed 50 new bookings in this segment, and I personally closed 10 of those deals. I helped guide my last company through the expansion into small businesses, and I'm eager to do that again at PopCo. Plus, I noticed you have a monthly karaoke night—so I'm eager to bring my rendition of 'Call Me Maybe' to the team as well."

What are your greatest strengths?

Here's an opening to talk about something that makes you great—and a great fit for this role. When you're answering this question, think quality, not quantity. In other words, don't rattle off a list of adjectives. Instead, pick one or a few (depending on the question) specific qualities that are relevant to this position and illustrate them with examples. Stories are always more memorable than generalizations. And if there's something you were hoping to mention because it makes you a great candidate, but you haven't had a chance yet, this would be the perfect time.

Possible answer to "What is your greatest strengths?"

"I'd say one of my greatest strengths is bringing organization to hectic environments and implementing processes to make everyone's lives easier. In my current role as an executive assistant to a CEO, I created new processes for pretty much everything, from scheduling meetings to planning monthly all hands agendas to preparing for event appearances. Everyone in the company knew how things worked and how long they would take, and the structures helped alleviate stress and set expectations on all sides. I'd be excited to bring that same approach to an operations manager role at a start-up, where everything is new and constantly growing and could use just the right amount of structure to keep things running smoothly."

What do you consider to be your weaknesses?

What your interviewer is really trying to do with this question—beyond identifying any major red flags—is to gauge your self-awareness and honesty. So, "I can't meet a deadline to save my life" is not an option—but neither is "Nothing! I'm perfect!" Strike a balance by thinking of something that you struggle with but that you're working to improve. For example, maybe you've never been strong at public speaking, but you've recently volunteered to run meetings to help you get more comfortable when addressing a crowd.

Possible answer to "What does you consider to be your weaknesses?"

"It can be difficult for me to gauge when the people I'm working with are overwhelmed or dissatisfied with their workloads. To ensure that I'm not asking too much or too little from my team, we have weekly check-ins. I like to ask if they feel like they're on top of their workload, how I could better support them, whether there's anything they'd like to take on or get rid of, and if they're engaged by what they're doing. Even if the answer is 'all good,' these meetings really lay the groundwork for a good and trusting relationship."

What is your greatest professional achievement?

Nothing says "hire me" better than a track record of achieving amazing results in past jobs, so don't be shy when answering this interview question! A great way to do so is by using the STAR method: situation, task, action, results. Set up the situation and the task that you were required to complete to provide the interviewer with background context (e.g., "In my last job as a junior analyst, it was my role to manage the invoicing process"), then describe what you did (the action) and what you achieved (the result): "In one month, I streamlined the process, which saved my group 10 person-hours each month and reduced errors on invoices by 25%."

Possible answer to "What is your greatest professional achievement?"

"My greatest accomplishment was when I helped the street lighting company, I worked for convince the small town of Bend, Oregon to convert antiquated street lighting to energy-efficient LED bulbs. My role was created to promote and sell the energy-efficient bulbs, while touting the long-term advantage of reduced energy costs. I had to develop a way to educate city light officials on the value of our energy-efficient bulbs—which was a challenge since our products had an expensive up-front cost compared to less efficient lighting options. I created an information packet and held local community events aimed at city officials and the tax-paying public. There, I was able to demo the company product, answer questions, and evangelize the value of LED bulbs for the long term. It was crucial to have the public on board and I was able to reach a wide variety of community members with these events. I not only reached my first-year sales goal of $100,000, but I was also able to help us land another contract in a neighboring city. Plus, the community-focused strategy garnered attention from the national media. And I'm proud to say I got a promotion within one year to senior sales representative.

Tell me about a challenge or conflict you've faced at work, and how you dealt with it.

You're probably not eager to talk about conflicts you've had at work during a job interview. But if you're asked directly, don't pretend you've never had one. Be honest about a difficult situation you've faced (but without going into the kind of detail you'd share venting to a friend). "Most people who ask are only looking for evidence that you're willing to face these kinds of issues head-on and make a sincere attempt at coming to a resolution," former recruiter Richard Moy says. Stay calm and professional as you tell the story (and answer any follow-up questions), spend more time talking about the resolution than the conflict, and mention what you'd do differently next time to show "you're open to learning from tough experiences."

Possible answer to "Tell me about a challenge or conflict you've faced at work, and how you dealt with it."

"Funnily enough, last year I was part of a committee that put together a training on conflict intervention in the workplace and the amount of pushback we got for requiring attendance really put our training to the test. There was one senior staff member in particular who seemed adamant. It took some careful listening to understand he felt like it wasn't the best use of his time given the workload he was juggling. I made sure to acknowledge his concern. And then I focused on his direct objection and explained how the training was meant to improve not just the culture of the company, but also the efficiency at which we operated—and that the goal was for the training to make everyone's workload feel lighter. He did eventually attend and was there when I talked to the whole staff about identifying the root issue of a conflict and addressing that directly without bringing in other issues, which is how I aim to handle any disagreement in the workplace."

Tell me about a challenge or conflict you've faced at work, and how you dealt with it.

You're probably not eager to talk about conflicts you've had at work during a job interview. But if you're asked directly, don't pretend you've never had one. Be honest about a difficult situation you've faced (but without going into the kind of detail you'd share venting to a friend). "Most people who ask are only looking for evidence that you're willing to face these kinds of issues head-on and make a sincere attempt at coming to a resolution," former recruiter Richard Moy says. Stay calm and professional as you tell the story (and answer any follow-up questions), spend more time talking about the resolution than the conflict, and mention what you'd do differently next time to show "you're open to learning from tough experiences."

Possible answer to "Tell me about a challenge or conflict you've faced at work, and how you dealt with it."

"Funnily enough, last year I was part of a committee that put together a training on conflict intervention in the workplace and the amount of pushback we got for requiring attendance really put our training to the test. There was one senior staff member in particular who seemed adamant. It took some careful listening to understand he felt like it wasn't the best use of his time given the workload he was juggling. I made sure to acknowledge his concern. And then I focused on his direct objection and explained how the training was meant to improve not just the culture of the company, but also the efficiency at which we operated—and that the goal was for the training to make everyone's workload feel lighter. He did eventually attend and was there when I talked to the whole staff about identifying the root issue of a conflict and addressing that directly without bringing in other issues, which is how I aim to handle any disagreement in the workplace."

What's a time you disagreed with a decision that was made at work?

The ideal anecdote here is one where you handled a disagreement professionally and learned something from the experience. Zhang recommends paying particular attention to how you start and end your response. To open, make a short statement to frame the rest of your answer, one that nods at the ultimate takeaway or the reason you're telling this story. For example: "I learned early on in my professional career that it's fine to disagree if you can back up your hunches with data." And to close strong, you can either give a one-sentence summary of your answer ("In short…") or talk briefly about how what you learned or gained from this experience would help you in the role you're interviewing for.

Possible answer to "What's a time you disagreed with a decision that was made at work?"

"In my job as a finance assistant, I was in charge of putting together reports for potential company investments. It was important to get the details and numbers right so that leaders had the best information to make a decision. One time, my boss asked me to generate a new report on a Wednesday morning and wanted it done by Thursday at 5 PM. Because I'm committed to high-quality work and I wasn't sure my boss fully understood what goes into each report, I knew I needed to speak up. At her next available opening, I sat down with my boss and explained my concerns. She was firm that the report would be completed by Thursday at 5 PM. So I decided to ask if there was anyone who could help out. After thinking about it, my boss found another assistant who could put in a few hours. While it was a tight timeline, we got the report done, and the committee was really pleased to review it at the meeting. My boss appreciated my extra efforts to make it happen and I felt good that I hadn't let the quality of the report slip. It was a good experience of being a team player but also knowing when and how to ask for help. And once I explained how much time and work goes into each report, my boss was careful to assign them further in advance."

What's a time you disagreed with a decision that was made at work?

The ideal anecdote here is one where you handled a disagreement professionally and learned something from the experience. Zhang recommends paying particular attention to how you start and end your response. To open, make a short statement to frame the rest of your answer, one that nods at the ultimate takeaway or the reason you're telling this story. For example: "I learned early on in my professional career that it's fine to disagree if you can back up your hunches with data." And to close strong, you can either give a one-sentence summary of your answer ("In short…")

or talk briefly about how what you learned or gained from this experience would help you in the role you're interviewing for.

Possible answer to "What's a time you disagreed with a decision that was made at work?"

"In my job as a finance assistant, I was in charge of putting together reports for potential company investments. It was important to get the details and numbers right so that leaders had the best information to make a decision. One time, my boss asked me to generate a new report on a Wednesday morning and wanted it done by Thursday at 5 PM. Because I'm committed to high-quality work and I wasn't sure my boss fully understood what goes into each report, I knew I needed to speak up. At her next available opening, I sat down with my boss and explained my concerns. She was firm that the report would be completed by Thursday at 5 PM. So I decided to ask if there was anyone who could help out. After thinking about it, my boss found another assistant who could put in a few hours. While it was a tight timeline, we got the report done, and the committee was really pleased to review it at the meeting. My boss appreciated my extra efforts to make it happen and I felt good that I hadn't let the quality of the report slip. It was a good experience of being a team player but also knowing when and how to ask for help. And once I explained how much time and work goes into each report, my boss was careful to assign them further in advance."

Tell me about a time you failed.

This question is very similar to the one about making a mistake, and you should approach your answer in much the same way. Make sure you pick a real, actual failure you can speak honestly about. Start by making it clear to the interviewer how you define failure. For instance: "As a manager, I consider it a failure whenever I'm caught by surprise. I strive to know what's going on with my team and their work." Then situate your story in relation to that definition and explain what happened. Finally, don't forget to share what you learned. It's OK to fail—everyone does sometimes—but it's important to show that you took something from the experience.

Possible answer to "Tell me about a time you failed."

"As a team manager, I consider it a failure if I don't know what's going on with my staff and their work—basically if a problem catches me by surprise, then I've failed somewhere along the way. Even if the outcome is ultimately fine, it means I've left a team member unsupported at some point. A somewhat recent example would be this training we do every year for new project managers. Because it's an event that my team has run so many times, I didn't think to check in and had no idea a scheduling conflict was brewing into a full-on turf war with another team. The resolution actually ended up being a quick and easy conversation at the leadership team meeting, but had I just asked about it sooner it would never have been a problem to begin with. I definitely learned my lesson about setting reminders to check in about major projects or events even if they've been done dozens of times before."

Why are you leaving your current job?

This is a toughie, but one you can be sure you'll be asked. Definitely keep things positive—you have nothing to gain by being negative about your current employer. Instead, frame things in a way that shows that you're eager to take on new opportunities and that the role you're interviewing for is a better fit for you. For example, "I'd really love to be part of product development from beginning to end, and I know I'd have that opportunity here." And if you were let go from your most recent job? Keep it simple: "Unfortunately, I was let go," is a totally acceptable answer.

Possible answer to "Why are you leaving your current job?"

"I'm ready for the next challenge in my career. I loved the people I worked with and the projects I worked on, but at some point I realized I wasn't being challenged the way I used to be. Rather than let myself get too comfortable, I decided to pursue a position where I can continue to grow."

Why were you fired?

Of course, they may ask the follow-up question: Why were you let go? If you lost your job due to layoffs, you can simply say, "The company [reorganized/merged/was acquired] and unfortunately my [position/department] was eliminated." But what if you were fired for performance reasons? Your best bet is to be honest (the job-seeking world is small, after all). But it doesn't have to be a deal breaker. Frame it as a learning experience: Share how you've grown and how you approach your job and life now as a result. And if you can portray your growth as an advantage for this next job, even better.

Possible answer to "Why were you fired?"

"After working for XYZ Inc. for four years, there were some changes made to the amount of client calls we were expected to process per hour. I used the techniques we were taught after the change took effect, but didn't want our customer service to slip. Unfortunately, I wasn't consistently completing the required number of calls, and, as a result, I was let go. I felt really bad about this and in retrospect I could have done better sticking to the process that would have let me meet the per hour quota. But you've told me about the customer service standards and the volume expectations here, and I believe it won't be a problem."

Why was there a gap in your employment?

Maybe you were taking care of children or aging parents, dealing with health issues, or traveling the world. Maybe it just took you a long time to land the right job. Whatever the reason, you should be prepared to discuss the gap (or gaps) on your resume. Seriously, practice saying your answer out loud. The key is to be honest, though that doesn't mean you have to share more details than you're comfortable with. If there are skills or qualities you honed or gained in your time away from the workforce—whether through volunteer work, running a home, or responding to a personal crisis—you can also talk about how those would help you excel in this role.

Possible answer to "Why was there a gap in your employment?"

"I spent a number of years working at a company in a very demanding job, in which—as you'll see from my references—I was very successful. But I'd reached a stage in my career where I wanted to focus on my personal growth. The time I spent traveling taught me a lot about how to get along with people of all ages and cultures. Now I feel more than ready to jump back into my career with renewed energy and focus and I feel this role is the ideal way to do that."

Can you explain why you changed career paths?

Don't be thrown off by this question—just take a deep breath and explain to the hiring manager why you've made the career decisions you have. More importantly, give a few examples of how your past experience is transferable to the new role. This doesn't have to be a direct connection; in fact, it's often more impressive when a candidate can show how seemingly irrelevant experience is very relevant to the role.

Possible answer to "Can you explain why you changed career paths?"

"Ever since my brother was diagnosed with a heart condition, I've been training and running with him in your annual Heart Run to raise money for your organization and help support patients with expenses not covered by insurance. Each time, I've been struck by how truly dedicated and happy to be there your employees have been. So when I saw this posting for a fundraising role, it felt like it was meant to be. For the last 10 years of my career I've been an account executive for various SaaS companies, and I've really honed my skills when it comes to convincing organizations to make regular payments for something over the long-term. But I've been looking for a position in fundraising where I can use these skills to really help people and I'm highly motivated to do that with your organization."

What's your current salary?

It's now illegal for some or all employers to ask you about your salary history in several cities and states, including New York City; Louisville, North Carolina; California; and Massachusetts. But no matter where you live, it can be stressful to hear this question. Don't panic—there are several possible strategies you can turn to. For example, you can deflect the question, Muse career coach Emily Liou says, with a response like: "Before discussing any salary, I'd really like to learn more about what this role entails. I've done a lot of research on [Company] and I am certain if it's the right fit, we'll be able to agree on a number that's fair and competitive to both parties." You can also reframe the question around your salary expectations or requirements (see question 38) or choose to share the number if you think it will work in your favor.

Possible answer to "What's your current salary?"

"Before discussing any salary, I'd really like to learn more about what this role entails. I've done a lot of research on [Company] and I am certain if it's the right fit, we'll be able to agree on a number that's fair and competitive to both parties."

What do you like least about your job?

Tread carefully here! The last thing you want to do is let your answer devolve into a rant about how terrible your current company is or how much you hate your boss or that one coworker. The easiest way to handle this question with poise is to focus on an opportunity the role you're interviewing for offers that your current job doesn't. You can keep the conversation positive and emphasize why you're so excited about the job.

Possible answer to "What do you like least about your job?"

"In my current role, I'm responsible for drafting media lists to pitch. While I've developed a knack for this and can do it when it is necessary, I'm looking forward to a job that allows me to have a more hands-on role in working with media partners. That's one of the things that most excited me about your account supervisor position."

What are you looking for in a new position?

Hint: Ideally the same things that this position has to offer. Be specific.

Possible answer to "What is you looking for in a new position?"

"I've been honing my data analysis skills for a few years now and, first and foremost, I'm looking for a position where I can continue to exercise those skills. Another thing that's important to me is the chance to present my findings and suggestions directly to clients. I'm always very motivated by being able to see the impact of my work on other people. And I'm definitely looking for a position where I can grow since I hope to take on managerial responsibilities in the future. To sum it up, I'd love a position where I can use my skills to make an impact that I can see with my own eyes. Of course, the position is only part of the equation. Being at a company where I can grow and work toward something I care about matters, too. DNF's goal of being at the intersection between data and education inspires me, and I'm really excited about this opportunity."

What type of work environment do you prefer?

Hint: Ideally one that's similar to the environment of the company you're applying to. Be specific.

Possible answer to "What type of work environment do you prefer?"

"I really like the environment in my current position. My manager is a great resource and always willing to help out when I run into an issue, but they trust me to get my work done so I have a lot of freedom in how I schedule and prioritize, which is very important to me. Everyone has their own cubicle, so it's often pretty quiet to get our work done, but we all get lunch together and our team has a lot of check-in meetings and communicates frequently via Slack so we still get a lot of opportunities to bounce ideas off each other. So I like both individual and more collaborative work. How would you describe the mix here?"

What's your work style?

When an interviewer asks you about your work style, they're probably trying to imagine you in the role. How will you approach your work? What will it be like to work with you? Will you mesh well with the existing team? You can help them along by choosing to focus on something that's important to you and aligns with everything you've learned about the role, team, and company so far. The question is broad, which means you have a lot of flexibility in how you answer: You might talk about how you communicate and collaborate on cross-functional projects, what kind of remote work setup allows you to be most productive, or how you approach leading a team and managing direct reports. Just try to keep it positive. And remember, telling a story will almost always make your answer more memorable.

Possible answer to "What's your work style?"

"I tend to do my best work when I'm collaborating with colleagues and we're working together toward a common goal. I was that rare student who loved group projects and now I still get a rush of excitement when I'm planning marketing campaigns with a team and bringing new and different voices into the fold. When I was working at XYZ Agency, I made it a habit to extend invitations to folks in different departments to join certain brainstorming and feedback sessions. Some of our most successful campaigns grew out of the ideas we generated together with co-workers in IT, HR, product, and customer success. That's why I was so excited to learn that this role would have me working closely with the product and sales teams as well as with a talented marketing team. The other thing I find is crucial to making these collaborations successful is organization and documentation, so I'm also really big on creating one central home for all materials related to a project, including meeting notes, action items, drafts of campaign copy and visuals, and timelines."

What's your management style?

The best managers are strong but flexible, and that's exactly what you want to show off in your answer. (Think something like, "While every situation and every team member requires a bit of a different strategy, I tend to approach my employee relationships as a coach...") Then share a couple of your best managerial moments, like when you grew your team from five to 15 or coached an underperforming employee to become the company's top salesperson.

Possible answer to "What's your management style?"

"Management style is so hard to put your finger on, but I think in general a good manager gives clear directions and actually stays pretty hands-off, but is ready and available to jump in to offer guidance, expertise, and help when needed. I try my best to make that my management style. I also go out of my way to make sure I know when my team needs help. That means plenty of informal check-ins, both on the work they're doing and on their general job satisfaction and mental well-being. I remember one project in particular at my most recent position that involved everyone working on a separate aspect of the product. This meant a lot of independent work for my team of seven people, but rather than bog everyone down with repetitive meetings to update me and everyone else on progress made, I created a project wiki that allowed us to communicate new information, when necessary, without disrupting another team member's work. I then made it my job to make sure no one was ever stuck on a problem too long without a sounding board. Ultimately, despite the disparate project responsibilities, we ended up with a very cohesive product and, more importantly, a team that wasn't burnt out."

How would your boss and co-workers describe you?

First, be honest (remember, if you make it to the final round, the hiring manager will be calling your former bosses and co-workers for references!). Then try to pull out strengths and traits you haven't discussed in other aspects of the interview, such as your strong work ethic or your willingness to pitch in on other projects when needed.

Possible answer to "How would your boss and co-workers describes you?"

"Actually, in my most recent performance review in April, my direct supervisor described me as someone who takes initiative and doesn't shy away from hard problems. My role involves a lot of on-site implementations, and when things go wrong, it's usually up to me to fix it. Rather than punting the problem back to the team, I always try to do what I can first. I know she appreciates that about me."

How do you deal with pressure or stressful situations?

Here's another question you may feel the urge to sidestep in an effort to prove you're the perfect candidate who can handle anything. But it's important not to dismiss this one (i.e. don't say, "I just put my head down and push through it," or, "I don't get stressed out"). Instead, talk about your go-to strategies for dealing with stress (whether it's meditating for 10 minutes every day or making sure you go for a run or keeping a super-detailed to-do list) and how you communicate and otherwise proactively try to mitigate pressure. If you can give a real example of a stressful situation, you navigated successfully, all the better.

Possible answer to "How do you deal with pressure or stressful situations?"

"I stay motivated by thinking about the end result. I've found that even in the midst of a challenging situation, reminding myself of my goals helps me take a step back and stay positive."

What do you like to do outside of work?

Interviewers will sometimes ask about your hobbies or interests outside of work in order to get to know you a little better—to find out what you're passionate about and devote time to during your off-hours. It's another chance to let your personality shine. Be honest, but keep it professional and be mindful of answers that might make it sound like you're going to spend all your time focusing on something other than the job you're applying for.

Possible answer to "What does you like to do outside of work?"

"I'm a huge foodie. My friends and I love trying new restaurants in town as soon as they open—the more unusual the better! I love discovering new foods and cuisines, and it's also a great activity to share with friends. I try to go out with the same group at least once a week and it's a fun way to make sure we keep in touch and share experiences even when we're busy with other things. We even took a trip to New York City and spent each day in a different neighbourhood, buying something to share from a few restaurants."

Are you planning on having children?

Questions about your family status, gender ("How would you handle managing a team of all men?"), nationality ("Where were you born?"), religion, or age are illegal—but they still get asked (and frequently). Of course, not always with ill intent—the interviewer might just be trying to make conversation and might not realize these are off-limits—but you should definitely tie any questions about your personal life (or anything else you think might be inappropriate) back to the job at hand.

Possible answer to "Are you planning on having children?"

"You know, I'm not quite there yet. But I am very interested in the career paths at your company. Can you tell me more about that?"

How do you prioritize your work?

Your interviewers want to know that you can manage your time, exercise judgement, communicate, and shift gears when needed. Start by talking about whatever system you've found works for you to plan your day or week, whether it's a to-do list app you swear by or a color-coded spreadsheet. This is one where you'll definitely want to lean on a real-life example. So go on to describe how you've reacted to a last-minute request or another unexpected shift in priorities in the past, incorporating how you evaluated and decided what to do and how you communicated with your manager and/or teammates about it.

Possible answer to "How do you prioritize your work?"

"I'd be lost without my daily to-do list! At the beginning of each workday, I write out tasks to complete, and list them from highest to lowest priority to help keep me on track. But I also realize priorities change unexpectedly. On one particular day recently, I had planned to spend most of my time making phone calls to advertising agencies to get price quotes for an upcoming campaign. Then I did a quick check-in with my manager. She mentioned she needed help putting together a presentation ASAP for a major potential client. I moved the more flexible task to the end of the week and spent the next few hours updating the time-sensitive presentation. I make it a point to keep lines of communication open with my manager and coworkers. If I'm working on a task that will take a while to complete, I try to give a heads-up to my team as soon as possible. If my workload gets to be unmanageable, I check in with my boss about which items can drop to the bottom of the priority list, and then I try to reset expectations about different deadlines."

What are you passionate about?

You're not a robot programmed to do your work and then power down. You're a human, and if someone asks you this question in an interview, it's probably because they want to get to know you better. The answer can align directly with the type of work you'd be doing in that role—like if, for example, you're applying to be a graphic designer and spend all of your free time creating illustrations and data visualizations to post on Instagram.

But don't be afraid to talk about a hobby that's different from your day-to-day work. Bonus points if you can "take it one step further and connect how your passion would make you an excellent candidate for the role you are applying for," says Muse career coach Al Dea. Like if you're a software developer who loves to bake, you might talk about how the ability to be both creative and precise informs your approach to code.

Possible answer to "What are you passionate about?"

"One of my favorite pastimes is knitting—I love being able to create something beautiful from nothing. Of course, knitting also requires a keen attention to detail and a lot of patience. Luckily, as an accountant I have cultivated both of those qualities!"

What are your pet peeves?

Here's another one that feels like a minefield. But it'll be easier to navigate if you know why an interviewer is asking it. Most likely, they want to make sure you'll thrive at their company—and get a glimpse of how you deal with conflict. So be certain you pick something that doesn't contradict the culture and environment at this organization while still being honest. Then explain why and what you've done to address it in the past, doing your best to stay calm and composed. Since there's no need to dwell on something that annoys you, you can keep this response short and sweet.

Possible answer to "What are your pet peeves?"

"It bothers me when an office's schedule is really disorganized, because in my experience, disorganization can cause confusion, which can hurt the motivation of the team. As a person who likes things to be orderly, I try to help keep my team on task while also allowing for flexibility."

What motivates you?

Before you panic about answering what feels like a probing existential question, consider that the interviewer wants to make sure you're excited about this role at this company, and that you'll be motivated to succeed if they pick you. So think back to what has energized you in previous roles and pinpoint what made your eyes light up when you read this job description. Pick one thing, make sure it's relevant to the role and company you're interviewing for, and try to weave in a story to help illustrate your point. If you're honest, which you should be, your enthusiasm will be palpable.

Possible answer to "What motivates you?"

"I'm driven primarily by my desire to learn new things—big or small—and take on new responsibilities so that I'm constantly growing as an employee and contributing more to my team and organization. I spent several summers working as a camp counsellor and felt most fulfilled when I volunteered to lead planning for a talent show, jumped in to help with scheduling logistics, and learned how to run pickups efficiently. All of that experience helped immensely when I took a step up to become the lead counsellor last year focused on operations, and that's what excites me so much about the opportunity to take on this managerial role for the after-school program."

How do you like to be managed?

This is another one of those questions that's about finding the right fit—both from the company's perspective and your own. Think back on what worked well for you in the past and what didn't. What did previous bosses do that motivated you and helped you succeed and grow? Pick one or two things to focus on and always articulate them with a positive framing (even if your preference comes from an experience where your manager behaved in the opposite way, phrase it as what you would want a manager to do). If you can give a positive example from a great boss, it'll make your answer even stronger.

Possible answer to "How do you like to be managed?"

"I enjoy having my hands in a lot of different projects, so I like working with managers who allow their employees to experiment, be independent, and work cross-functionally with other teams. At the same time, I really welcome it when a boss provides me with support, guidance, and coaching.

Do you consider yourself successful?

This question might make you uncomfortable. But you can think of it as an opportunity to allow the interviewer to get to know you better and to position yourself as an excellent choice for this job. First off, make sure you say yes! Then pick one specific professional achievement you're proud of that can be tied back to the role you're interviewing for—one that demonstrates a quality, skill, or experience that would help you excel in this position. You'll want to explain why you consider it a success, talk about the process in addition to the outcome, and highlight your own accomplishment without forgetting your team. Zooming in on one story will help if you feel awkward tooting your own horn!

Possible answer to "Do you consider yourself successful?"

"I do consider myself successful, even though I'm early in my professional career. I took a full load of classes in my junior year of college because I wanted to take that summer to volunteer for a human rights organization overseas. I knew that I needed to make sure I was on track with my major, minor, and graduation requirements. It was difficult to juggle it all with my part-time job, which I kept to help account for the fact that I wouldn't be earning money over the summer, and there were a few sleepless nights. But it was worth the hard work: I ended the year with a 3.9 GPA and the opportunity to volunteer for the agency in Ghana without falling behind my graduation timeline. For me success is about setting a goal and sticking with it, no matter how hard it is, and this experience was proof that I could be successful even when there's a lot to balance, which I know there always is at a non-profit like this one."

Where do you see yourself in five years?

If asked this question, be honest and specific about your future goals, but consider this: A hiring manager wants to know a) if you've set realistic expectations for your career, b) if you have ambition (a.k.a., this interview isn't the first time you're considering the question), and c) if the position aligns with your goals and growth. Your best bet is to think realistically about where this position could take you and answer along those lines. And if the position isn't necessarily a one-way ticket to your aspirations? It's OK to say that you're not quite sure what the future holds, but that you see this experience playing an important role in helping you make that decision.

Possible answer to "Where do you see yourself in five years?"

"In five years, I'd like to be in a position where I know more about my longer-term career aspirations as a designer. I will have gotten experience working for a design agency and know more about the industry overall. I'll have grown my technical skills and learned how to take feedback from clients and incorporate it. And the way your agency is set up, I'll also have gotten the opportunity to design different kinds of deliverables—including websites, branding, and ad campaigns—for different kinds of clients to see where I really feel at home before settling on a focus."

How do you plan to achieve your career goals?

Having goals shows interviewers you care, are ambitious, and can think ahead. Having a plan for how you'll achieve your goals demonstrates your self-motivation as well as organizational and time management skills. Finally, the fact that you've accomplished past goals you've set for yourself is proof of your ability to follow through. All together, these are indications that you can not only set and achieve goals of your own, but also help your prospective boss, team, and company do the same. To craft your answer, make sure you focus on one or two goals in detail, explain why the goals are meaningful, communicate what milestones are coming up, highlight past successes, and connect back to this job.

Possible answer to "How do you plan to achieve your career goals?"

"My current goal is to earn the CPA license so that I'm fully certified and prepared to contribute in a junior staff accounting job. My undergraduate degree is in finance and I completed an accounting internship with XYZ Company last summer. While I was there, I decided that each week I'd ask one person from a different team to coffee to learn about their job and career path. Not only did those conversations impress upon me the importance of getting my CPA as soon as possible, they also helped me realize I was eager to pursue forensic accounting, which is why I'm so excited about the opportunity to join this team. In order to ensure I earn my CPA this year, I enrolled in NASBA workshops, created a study schedule to keep myself on track, and will be taking my first trial test in three weeks. I plan on taking the actual test within the next three to six months."

What are your career aspirations?

Career aspirations are bigger and loftier than career goals. With this question, interviewers are asking: What kind of career would make you happiest (while also being realistic)? Your aspirations might revolve around what kind of company you'd like to work for, what tasks you'd like to do, who you'd like to help, or how you'd like to be seen by your colleagues. So to answer this question, talk about what would energize and fulfil you and connect it to the position you're interviewing for. Be specific about how this job will help you achieve your career aspirations.

Possible answer to "What is your career aspirations?"

"After growing up in a food desert, my biggest professional aspiration is to help make healthy food more widely available and accessible regardless of where you live. I also love solving complex problems. Currently, as a project manager, I specialize in strategic planning and combine it with a natural ability to engage critical stakeholders—resulting in on-time and under-budget delivery. This role would help me use those skills to work on a mission I'm passionate about. I am determined to use these skills to help your organization guarantee our community has access to affordable, nutritious food and information to make healthy decisions. In the next five or so years, I would love to take on additional responsibility and be in a decision-making role to drive the mission beyond our community and support even more families in gaining access to nutritious food options."

What's your dream job?

Along similar lines, the interviewer wants to uncover whether this position is really in line with your ultimate career goals. While "an NBA star" might get you a few laughs, a better bet is to talk about your goals and ambitions—and why this job will get you closer to them.

What other companies are you interviewing with?

Companies might ask you who else you're interviewing with for a few reasons. Maybe they want to see how serious you are about this role and team (or even this field) or they're trying to find out who they're competing with to hire you. On one hand, you want to express your enthusiasm for this job, but at the same time, you don't want to give the company any more leverage than it already has by telling them there's no one else in the running. Depending on where you are in your search, you can talk about applying to or interviewing for a few roles that have XYZ in common—then mention how and why this role seems like a particularly good fit.

Possible answer to "What other companies are you interviewing with?"

"I'm interviewing with a few companies for a range of positions, but they all come down to delivering an excellent customer experience. I wanted to keep an open mind about how to best achieve that goal, but so far it seems that this role will really allow me to focus all of my energy on customer experience and retention, which I find very appealing."

What makes you unique?

"They genuinely want to know the answer," DEA promises. Give them a reason to pick you over other similar candidates. The key is to keep your answer relevant to the role you're applying to. So the fact that you can run a six-minute mile or crush a trivia challenge might not help you get the job (but hey, it depends on the job!). Use this opportunity to tell them something that would give you an edge over your competition for this position. To figure out what that is, you can ask some former colleagues, think back to patterns you've seen in feedback you get, or try to distil why people tend to turn to you. Focus on one or two things and don't forget to back up whatever you say with evidence.

Possible answer to "What makes you unique?"

"I basically taught myself animation from scratch. I was immediately drawn to it in college, and with the limited resources available to me, I decided to take matters into my own hands—and that's the approach I take in all aspects of my work as a video editor. I don't just wait around for things to happen, and when I can, I'm always eager to step in and take on new projects, pick up new skills, or brainstorm new ideas."

What should I know that's not on your resume?

It's a good sign if a recruiter or hiring manager is interested in more than just what's on your resume. It probably means they looked at your resume, think you might be a good fit for the role, and want to know more about you. To make this wide-open question a little more manageable, try talking about a positive trait, a story or detail that reveals a little more about you and your experience, or a mission or goal that makes you excited about this role or company.

Possible answer to "What should I know that's not on your resume?"

"Well, one thing you won't find on my resume: the time I had to administer emergency CPR. Last year, I was at the lake when I saw a young girl who looked like she was drowning. I was a lifeguard in high school, so I swam out, brought her to shore, and gave her CPR. Although this was—hopefully—a one-time event, I've always been able to stay calm during stressful situations, figure out a solution, and then act. As your account manager, I'd use this trait to quickly and effectively resolve issues both within the team and externally. After all, obstacles are inevitable, especially in a start-up environment. And if anyone needs CPR at the office beach party, well, I'm your woman."

What would your first few months look like in this role?0

Your potential future boss (or whoever else has asked you this question) wants to know that you've done your research, given some thought to how you'd get started, and would be able to take initiative if hired. (In some interviews, you might even get the more specific, "What would your first 30, 60, or 90 days look like in this role?") So think about what information and aspects of the company and team you'd need to familiarize yourself with and which colleagues you'd want to sit down and talk to. You can also suggest one possible starter project to show you'd be ready to hit the ground running and contribute early on. This won't necessarily be the thing you do first if you do get the job, but a good answer shows that you're thoughtful and that you care.

Possible answer to "What would your first few months look like in this role?"

"It's been exciting to hear about some of the new initiatives the company has started in our previous conversations—like the database project and the company-wide sync, but I know there's still a lot for me to learn. The first thing I'd do is line up meetings with the stakeholders involved in the projects I'd be tackling to help me figure out what I don't know and then go from there. Hopping into a database project halfway through can be tricky, but I'm confident that once I know what all the stakeholders are looking for, I'll be able to efficiently plot out our next steps and set appropriate deadlines. From there, I'll be focused on hitting the milestones that I've set for the team."

What are your salary expectations?

The number one rule of answering this question is: Figure out your salary requirements ahead of time. Do your research on what similar roles pay by using sites like PayScale and reaching out to your network. Be sure to take your experience, education, skills, and personal needs into account, too! From there, Muse career coach Jennifer Fink suggests choosing from one of three strategies:

Give a salary range: But keep the bottom of your stated range toward the mid-to-high point of what you're actually hoping for, Fink says.

Flip the question: Try something like "That's a great question—it would be helpful if you could share what the range is for this role," Fink says.

Delay answering: Tell your interviewer that you'd like to learn more about the role or the rest of the compensation package before discussing pay.

Possible answer to "What are your salary expectations?"

"Taking into account my experience and Excel certifications, which you mentioned earlier would be very helpful to the team, I'm looking for somewhere between $42,000 and $46,000 annually for this role. But for me, benefits definitely matter as well. Your free on-site gym, the commuter benefits, and other perks could definitely allow me to be a bit flexible with salary."

What do you think we could do better or differently?

This question can really do a number on you. How do you give a meaty answer without insulting the company or, worse, the person you're speaking with? Well first, take a deep breath. Then start your response with something positive about the company or specific product you've been asked to discuss. When you're ready to give your constructive feedback, give some background on the perspective you're bringing to the table and explain why you'd make the change you're suggesting (ideally based on some past experience or other evidence). And if you end with a question, you can show them you're curious about the company or product and open to other points of view. Try: "Did you consider that approach here? I'd love to know more about your process."

When can you start?

Your goal here should be to set realistic expectations that will work for both you and the company. What exactly that sounds like will depend on your specific situation. If you're ready to start immediately—if you're unemployed, for example—you could offer to start within the week. But if you need to give notice to your current employer, don't be afraid to say so; people will understand and respect that you plan to wrap things up right. It's also legitimate to want to take a break between jobs, though you might want to say you have "previously scheduled commitments to attend to" and try to be flexible if they really need someone to start a bit sooner.

Possible answer to "When can you start?"

"I am excited for the opportunity to join your team. I have several projects to wrap up in my current role at [Company]. I plan to give them two weeks' notice to make a smooth transition for my coworkers and will be happy to come onboard with the team here after that time."

Are you willing to relocate?

While this may sound like a simple yes-or-no question, it's often a little bit more complicated than that. The simplest scenario is one where you're totally open to moving and would be willing to do so for this opportunity. But if the answer is no, or at least not right now, you can reiterate your enthusiasm for the role, briefly explain why you can't move at this time, and offer an alternative, like working remotely or out of a local office. Sometimes it's not as clear-cut, and that's OK. You can say you prefer to stay put for xyz reasons, but would be willing to consider relocating for the right opportunity.

Possible answer to "Are you willing to relocate?"

"I do love living in Raleigh and would prefer to stay here. However, for the right opportunity I'd be willing to consider relocating if necessary."

How many tennis balls can you fit into a limousine?

1,000? 10,000? 100,000? Seriously? Well, seriously, you might get asked brain-teaser questions like these, especially in quantitative jobs. But remember that the interviewer doesn't necessarily want an exact number—they want to make sure that you understand what's being asked of you, and that you can set into motion a systematic and logical way to respond. So take a deep breath and start thinking through the math. (Yes, it's OK to ask for a pen and paper!)

If you were an animal, which one would you want to be?

Seemingly random personality-test type questions like these come up in interviews because hiring managers want to see how you can think on your feet. There's no wrong answer here, but you'll immediately gain bonus points if your answer helps you share your strengths or personality or connect with the hiring manager. Pro tip: Come up with a stalling tactic to buy yourself some thinking time, such as saying, "Now, that is a great question. I think I would have to say..."

Sell me this pen.

If you're interviewing for a sales job, your interviewer might put you on the spot to sell them a pen sitting on the table, or a legal pad, or a water bottle, or just something. The main thing they're testing you for? How you handle a high-pressure situation. So try to stay calm and confident and use your body language—making eye contact, sitting up straight, and more—to convey that you can handle this. Make sure you listen, understand your "customer's" needs, get specific about the item's features and benefits, and end strong—as though you were truly closing a deal.

Is there anything else you'd like us to know?

Just when you thought you were done, your interviewer asks you this open-ended doozy. Don't panic—it's not a trick question! You can use this as an opportunity to close out the meeting on a high note in one of two ways, Zhang says. First, if there really is something relevant that you haven't had a chance to mention, do it now. Otherwise, you can briefly summarize your qualifications. For example, Zhang says, you could say: "I think we've covered most of it, but just to summarize, it sounds like you're looking for someone who can really hit the ground running. And with my previous experience [enumerate experience here], I think I'd be a great fit."

Do you have any questions for us?

You probably already know that an interview isn't just a chance for a hiring manager to grill you—it's an opportunity to sniff out whether a job is the right fit from your perspective. What do you want to know about the position? The company? The department? The team? You'll cover a lot of this in the actual interview, so have a few less-common questions ready to go. We especially like questions targeted to the interviewer ("What's your favorite part about working here?") or the company's growth ("What can you tell me about your new products or plans for growth?") If you're interviewing for a remote role, there are some specific questions you might want to ask related to that.

CHAPTER THIRTEEN

Type of Interview

Interviews come in all shapes and sizes: Sometimes you're with one interviewer, others you're with five. Maybe you'll be asked to lunch, expected to solve a problem, or invited to a Skype interview.

But no matter what the format, we'll give you what you need to succeed.

The Traditional Interview

This is the scenario you'll face most often: You sit down with a solo interviewer and answer a series of questions designed to help her figure out if you're a great candidate for the job.

The Phone Interview

Asked for a phone interview? A call is typically a first-round screening to see if you're a fit to come in for a full interview, so nailing it is key. You'll want to prepare just as you would for an in-person interview, with some key adjustments for the phone format.

The Video Interview

Video interviews take the phone-screening interview to the next level, and they're becoming a regular part of the job application process for many companies. From choosing the right on-screen look to making sure all of your tech systems are a go, you'll want to be 100% ready.

. The Case Interview

The case interview is a more specialized format in which you're given a business problem ("How can BigCoal Co. double its growth?") or a puzzle ("How many tennis balls fit in a 747?") to solve. While case interviews were once exclusively the domain of aspiring consultants, they're now popping up everywhere from tech companies to NGOs.

The Puzzle Interview

Google and other highly competitive companies have been known to ask "puzzle" questions, like, "How many people are using Facebook in San Francisco at 2:30 PM on a Friday?" Seems random, but your interviewer wants to determine how quickly you can think on your feet, how you'll approach a difficult situation, and how you can make progress in the face of a challenge.

The Lunch Interview

Has your potential employer suggested an interview over a meal? That's a good sign—it usually means she wants to learn a little more about you and how you act outside of the office. We'll show how to highlight your strengths and accomplishments while trying to maneuver a mouthful of chicken Piccata.

The Group Interview

Group interviews aren't common, but you might find them for sales roles, internships, or other positions in which the company is hiring multiple people for the same job. How do you catch the hiring manager's eye when your part of the group? It takes a little gusto and a few smart tactics.

The Working Interview

In some industries—writing, engineering, or even sales—you may be asked to complete an actual job task as part of the interview. Basically, your interviewers don't want you to tell them you can do the job, they want to see it.

Don't panic: If you go in prepared, this is your chance to shine.

. The Panel Interview

If you'll be reporting to several people or working with a team, it's not uncommon to meet with multiple interviewers—all at the same time. Sounds nice, because you only have to answer those tough questions once, but it can also be tricky to make a strong connection with each decision maker.

The Career Fair Interview

If you're attending career fairs as part of your job hunt, get ready for impromptu interviews, where you'll only have 10 or 15 minutes to sell yourself to the recruiter for a chance to come in for a full interview.

CHAPTER FOURTEEN

Tips To Clear Interview In st Attempt

Don't Be Nervous

Nervousness can be your biggest enemy in the Interview. Prepare well before and beat the nervousness. There is no use of being nervous, it is not a war, take is just like a simple interview, go like a roaring tiger and clear it!

Practice Makes Everyone Perfect

Practising will make you better and nearly perfect, it is advisable to practice for the Psych Tests well before, this is so because these tests are done under a very strict time constraint if you are practising for them in advance; it'll help you a lot in managing the time there. Also, practice speaking in English, it is very important that you are fluent enough in English to converse with the Interviewer and speak in GD and Lecturette.

The Coaching Dilemma

Many of us wonder whether or not to go for coaching. The answer is that if you are totally clueless about what the Interview Procedure is, you must surely attend good coaching. However, coaching is avoidable for those who have somebody to guide them, somebody who has good knowledge about Interview Procedure. Select the right academy keeping various things in mind.

The 'Be Positive' Funda

Interview is all about positive attitude, so be it your psych tests, interview, GT Series or anything else, be positive. Your personality should reflect that you are an assertive person, right from your answers in psych tests to your personality and behaviour in GT and Interview.

Friendliness With Your Group

Being friendly with your group is very important since there are almost 7-8 tasks which you have to do as a group and where it counts whether or not your group likes you. Since the testing is done in groups hence it is important that each one in your group likes you. Be friendly and non-judgmental towards others.

General Knowledge

You need to be aware of what is happening in your nation and in the world. Only superficial knowledge will not help, get to know the things in detail. Have strong viewpoints towards the cases and be ready for a good debate with the Interviewing officer on the GK things. Be a regular reader of the newspaper and don't miss even the minutest details.

Knowing Yourself and Things Around You

It is necessary for the interview that you know yourself well, be prepared with all the data about yourself, like your grades, achievements and good/bad qualities etc. In a similar manner, you must be aware of the details about your family like their occupation, good/bad points etc. Make sure that you know in details about your hobbies or the games you have played.

Dress Up

Your dress up is important in casting a good impression in front of others. Be careful about what you are choosing to wear. You have to be dressed appropriately according to the occasion. Hence choose your dress wisely; there are guidelines available for both men and women on what all they can wear in Interview

Physical Fitness

You have to undergo long hours of tasks which will be tiring and exhausting; however, you'll not realize this in the josh! You have to be physically fit since you have to do physical tasks as well. Be careful of the way you walk and sit, don't look lazy from your gait. If you'll be physically fit your personality will reflect that. It is advisable to do some running/light exercise regularly.

Overconfidence Will Make You Pay

Being confident is one thing and overconfident is completely opposite. Your overconfidence will eat up all your chances of success. Hence be confident but not overconfident

CHAPTER FIFTEEN

Motivational Quates for success in Interview.

Words of encouragement for a job interview are uplifting sayings that inspire you to reach your full potential and be persistent. Below are 62 quotes to help you in the final stage of your job hunt.

Quotes about being persistent

During an interview, you may be asked some challenging questions or be faced with a trial assignment that requires determination. These quotes about being persistent can help you to remember to try your best:

"If you're going through hell, keep going." — Winston Churchill

"Opportunities don't happen, you create them." — Chris Grosser

"The best way out is always through." — Robert Frost

"Don't be afraid to fail. Don't waste energy trying to cover up failure. Learn from your failures and go on to the next challenge." — H. Stanley Judd

"In the middle of difficulty lies opportunity." — Albert Einstein

"You miss 100% of the shots you don't take." — Wayne Gretzky

"It does not matter how slowly you go as long as you do not stop." — Confucius

"Trust yourself. You know more than you think you do." — Dr. Benjamin Spock

"Optimism is the faith that leads to achievement." — Helen Keller

"I believed, and still believe, that you can build your dreams brick by brick. That you can accomplish anything with persistence." — Maurene Goo

"There is only one way to avoid criticism: Do nothing, say nothing, and be nothing." — Elbert Hubbard

"It's not whether you get knocked down. It's whether you get up." — Vince Lombardi

"A mind troubled by doubt cannot focus on the course to victory." — Arthur Golden

"There are no shortcuts to any place worth going." — Beverly Sills

"One important key to success is self-confidence. An important key to self-confidence is preparation." — Arthur Ashe

"I am convinced that life is 10% what happens to me and 90% of how I react to it." — Charles Swindoll

"Success is not final; failure is not fatal: it is the courage to continue that counts." — Winston Churchill

Quotes about taking risks

Since interviewing for a job can sometimes mean you are changing career paths or are starting something new, it's important to remember the benefit of taking risks. These quotes encourage you to venture into the unknown:

"Don't be afraid to go out on a limb. That's where the fruit is." — H. Jackson Brown

"You can't be that kid standing at the top of the waterslide, overthinking it. You have to go down the chute." — Tina Fey

"Your current safe boundaries were once unknown frontiers." — Anonymous

"There is a way to do it better — find it." — Thomas Edison

"Life shrinks or expands in proportion to one's courage." — Anais Nin

"When I let go of what I am, I become what I might be." — Lao Tzu

"Believe in yourself! Have faith in your abilities! Without a humble but reasonable confidence in your own powers, you cannot be successful or happy." — Norman Vincent Peale

"Only those who dare to fail greatly can ever achieve greatly." — Robert F. Kennedy

"Step out of the history that is holding you back. Step into the new story you are willing to create." — Oprah Winfrey

"A coward gets scared and quits. A hero gets scared, but still goes on." — Anonymous

Quotes about seeking opportunities

Job interviews are about finding opportunities to showcase your professional skills and experiences to potential employers. Here are some opportunity-seeking quotes to encourage you in considering this interview as the start of your next career:

"The question isn't who's going to let me; it's who's going to stop me." — Ayn Rand

"Never put off for tomorrow what you can do today." — Thomas Jefferson

"If you are insecure, guess what? The rest of the world is too. Do not overestimate the competition and underestimate yourself. You are better than you think." — T. Harv Eker

"The future depends on what you do today." — Mahatma Gandhi

"To improve is to change; to be perfect is to change often." — Winston Churchill

"If you're offered a seat on a rocket ship, don't ask what seat! Just get on." — Sheryl Sandberg

"The way to get started is to quit talking and begin doing." — Walt Disney

"True life is lived when tiny changes occur." — Leo Tolstoy

"Start by doing what is necessary, then what is possible, and suddenly you are doing the impossible." — Francis of Assisi

"If it scares you, it might be a good thing to try." — Seth Godin

Quotes about following your dreams

Interviewing for a job can be the first step to making your career dreams a reality. Use these quotes about following your dreams to remind you that it's possible to find your ideal career:

"Find out what you like doing best, and get someone to pay you for it." — Katharine Whitehorn

"Whether you think you can or you think you can't, you're right." — Henry Ford

"The future belongs to those who believe in the beauty of their dreams." — Eleanor Roosevelt

"It is never too late to be what you might have been." — George Eliot

"Doubt kills more dreams than failure ever will." — Karim Seddiki

"Whatever you decide to do, make sure it makes you happy." — Paulo Coelho

"Be yourself; everyone else is already taken." — Oscar Wilde

"Act as if what you do makes a difference. It does." — William James

"Without leaps of imagination, or dreaming, we lose the excitement of possibilities. Dreaming, after all, is a form of planning." — Gloria Steinem

"Be bold enough to use your voice, brave enough to listen to your heart and strong enough to live the life you've always imagined." — Anonymous

"A big name or a big designation doesn't make a man big but responsibilities do." — Vikash Shrivastava

"What's the point of being alive if you don't at least try to do something remarkable?" — John Green

"Whatever you are, be a good one." — Abraham Lincoln

"Too many of us are not living our dreams because we are living our fears." — Les Brown

Quotes about following your dreams

Interviewing for a job can be the first step to making your career dreams a reality. Use these quotes about following your dreams to remind you that it's possible to find your ideal career:

"Find out what you like doing best, and get someone to pay you for it." — Katharine Whitehorn

"Whether you think you can or you think you can't, you're right." — Henry Ford

"The future belongs to those who believe in the beauty of their dreams." — Eleanor Roosevelt

"It is never too late to be what you might have been." — George Eliot

"Doubt kills more dreams than failure ever will." — Karim Seddiki

"Whatever you decide to do, make sure it makes you happy." — Paulo Coelho

"Be yourself; everyone else is already taken." — Oscar Wilde

"Act as if what you do makes a difference. It does." — William James

"Without leaps of imagination, or dreaming, we lose the excitement of possibilities. Dreaming, after all, is a form of planning." — Gloria Steinem

"Be bold enough to use your voice, brave enough to listen to your heart and strong enough to live the life you've always imagined." — Anonymous

"A big name or a big designation doesn't make a man big but responsibilities do." — Vikash Shrivastava

"What's the point of being alive if you don't at least try to do something remarkable?" — John Green

"Whatever you are, be a good one." — Abraham Lincoln

"Too many of us are not living our dreams because we are living our fears." — Les Brown

THE END

www.ingramcontent.com/pod-product-compliance
Lightning Source LLC
Chambersburg PA
CBHW050801160726
48004CB00002B/651